S☉UL
REGRESSION
therapy

*Healing the Soul through Hypnotic Regression
To Past Lives and Between Life Experiences*

Lorna and John Jackson CHt, LBLt, SRTt.

SOUL REGRESSION THERAPY

First published in Australia by Spiritual Regression Australia PTY LTD 2016
http://thejacksoninstitute.com.au

*Catalogue-in-Publication details available from the
National Library of Australia*

ISBN: 978-0-9946062-0-4 (pbk)

This book is a work of non-fiction.

Also available as an ebook: 978-0-9946062-1-1 (ebk)

© Book layout design and typesetting by Publicious P/L
Published with the assistance of Publicious P/L
www.publicious.com.au

DISCLAIMER: This book includes original first-hand accounts from our clients who have personally remembered their own previous existence through hypnotic regression. Some of the details and places in these case studies have been verified by the subjects. All names have been changed to ensure they remain anonymous. All information provided in this book is designed to provide helpful information. While many of the case studies describe transformational outcomes no claims are made of any miraculous effectiveness. We also advice that no one should attempt to use the process of spiritual regression unless they are adequately trained by qualified professionals in this modality. Dates and places might not line up with historical facts, what is most important is the therapeutic part of the session, we are not looking for proof of reincarnation.

DEDICATION

We dedicate this book to all souls on Earth, whether they are therapists or healers who are either interested in knowing about their soul journey or feel the calling to become a Spiritual Regression facilitator. We also dedicate this book to the Universal Spirit, the giver of the Light and the Knowledge, for being given the privilege of receiving the insights and messages in order to create this book.

We Are a River

Our life has not been an ascent
up one side of a mountain and down the other.
We did not reach a peak,
only to decline and die.
We have been as drops of water,
born in the ocean and sprinkled on the earth in a gentle rain.
We became a spring,
and then a stream,
and finally a river flowing deeper and stronger, nourishing all it
touches as it nears its home once again.
*
Don't accept the modern myths of aging.
You are not declining.
You are not fading away into uselessness.
You are a sage,
a river at its deepest
and most nourishing.
Sit by a river bank some time
and watch attentively as the river
tells you of your life.

Lao Tzu, (William Martin's free-verse interpretation of *Tao Te Ching*)

Contents

INTRODUCTION

Over the many years in our work as Past Life and Between Life Regression therapists we have witnessed many life transforming occurrences, these have emerged from the clients we have seen in our clinic rooms and also at the trainings we regularly hold for Soul Regression Therapy. Many sessions were of sadness, trauma and grief and we feel blessed to be able to both facilitate and witness them. People have come to see us with the hope they can change the way they feel about their problems and let go of past emotional pains and physical symptoms that haunts them. Some people decide to enrol in our unique Soul Regression Therapy 6-day training program because they want to learn a new healing modality to include in their already existing tool box of therapies. Others decide to attend the training for their own personal and spiritual development.

As therapists we fully understand that we all have a soul story that is stored deep inside of us. Often we are unaware that a powerful healing has happened in a session until much later when the client sends an email or calls on the phone. There is a lot of information that comes from a session and often the person needs time to process and integrate the immortal information and insights they have gained.

This book contains many stories that have been carefully collected over the years of our work as therapists and from our training courses. We have decided to share them here to help the reader to not only understand the phenomena of Hypnotic Soul Regression Therapy, but to also understand the souls journey from one life to the next and how the spiritual realms operate. These stories show how pain, sorrow, grief and anger can be transformed into love, knowledge and wisdom and highlight important life lessons that many people are experiencing in the world today.

The terms afterlife, between life or between lives used in this book are interchangeable and refer to the place the soul transitions to after death occurs. This is the place where the soul goes to between incarnations and the place the soul calls home.

Whilst reading the case studies included in this book you may identify with some of the characters on a personal level and recognise facets of yourself and your own soul journey in their story. Reading the personal accounts of others in this book may begin to initiate healing or to inspire you to have a Soul Regression Therapy session for yourself with one of the many skilled people we have trained. Our clients past lives are really fascinating and we have kept detailed written and recorded records of all the sessions facilitated since the very first session (which is included in this book) Lorna nervously facilitated many years ago.

We kept the records not only for own learning and research purposes, but also with the thought that one day we would compile these case studies into a book that would help people to understand the benefits of this powerful healing therapy. And so this is the first in a series of books that John and Lorna intend to write about Soul Regression Therapy and the spiritual world which includes the fascinating subject of reincarnation, past lives and the afterlife. How the spiritual world affects and enriches the physical 3D world we live in and the choices we make.

There are many reasons people come for a Soul Regression Therapy session. Some come from curiosity, they may have heard about past life regression, read a book on the subject, seen a documentary on television or the internet. This triggers a curiosity inside of them to know if they can be hypnotised and regressed to remember their own previous lives lived. Or they may have a very serious problem they want to heal or resolve.

The aim of therapeutic hypnotic past life regression is to resolve unconscious patterns, contracts, agreements, and complexes such as fears or phobias that may come from past lives that are negatively affecting the present quality of life. By exploring our past lives we can see beyond the confusion and illusions of the present life to bring about a healing that can resonate into the present life. If in a past life you were a healer, in spiritual or religious service, you may have taken vows of poverty, chastity, obedience, silence or secrecy, or vows that prevented you from personally benefitting from healing energy, speaking up or having a fulfilling relationship. These vows or contracts may still be running unconsciously and affect relationships in the current life. Often the soul re-creates similar experiences from past lives in the present life, these experiences run unconsciously in the current life but are an attempt by the soul to complete or heal an unresolved past life experience.

An example and metaphor of repeating karma is the movie "Ground Hog Day", where Phil Connors played by actor Bill Murray keeps repeating 1 day in his life over and over, until he finally works out his lesson and changes his behavior and moves on. Once these negative patterns are uncovered they can be cleared. Past life regression can help us to know and understand that death is not a threat and will only destroy the physical body. The spirit or soul lives on and loved ones haven't been lost forever; they have merely travelled to another place. Past life regression can give purpose and meaning to life and can help to understand that each life is devised for learning not punishment. We learn more deeply from hardships and pain and regression therapy brings new perspectives and healing for individuals in a way no other therapy can achieve.

Often clients will go beyond the death in a past life to the afterlife, if this happens they are encouraged to keep going and to describe where they are, how they feel and what's happening. They may meet with spirit guides, Master guides or with the spirits of deceased loved ones. This experience is extremely profound and they may receive a healing or advice about their present life. Through an afterlife regression a person can discover who is in their soul family, who they are as an immortal soul and what their life purpose is. We have been extremely privileged to have witnessed the hidden realms and journeys of the immortal soul as it reincarnates from life to life and this has inspired us to share these transformational case studies with others.

Looking back on our lives now, we realise our path to becoming regression therapists was all part of extensive soul planning, intrinsically linking to our present lifetime together. We are extremely grateful, because through this work and the many sessions we have witnessed with our clients we have come to understand ourselves more deeply on a soul level, along with our place in this world and to know we are right on purpose. Along with understanding of the connection to family and through releasing many of own karmic patterns and complexes we now clearly realise the purpose of reincarnation is to rise above past limiting barriers and fears of past lives and move into the higher vibration of self-acceptance, love and forgiveness.

As we move into the Golden Age that was foreseen by the ancients, we are indeed in the dawning of the Age of Aquarius, the Earth and humanity are experiencing a vital shift of energy from a third to a fifth dimensional frequency. We firmly believe that we humans are moving into a cycle of new evolutionary growth and into a phase of limitless potential.

The Earth is experiencing a time of profound change, a coming of new wisdom and it is up to us as individuals take up the challenge for our own personal healing, self-responsibility and empowerment. As we do this our actions will have a ripple effect and touch everyone we come into contact with. The more we each awaken to our personal contribution in this shift of consciousness energy, the greater the possibilities will emerge for positive change on our planet Earth.

We are here to stretch ourselves beyond our previous limits and lifetimes. We are here to inspire others to do the same, so that humanity breaks through the stagnant ways of previous generations moving forward to newer and ever more magnificent ways of being, doing and having. Most people try to help make the world a better place, and this is part of our legacy to the present and beyond and we are truly honoured and blessed to be of service when called to do so.

Our training and professional experience has led us to co-create a revolutionary process of hypnotic regression we call Soul Regression Therapy. This therapy includes a blending of past life regression therapy and regression to the afterlife using powerful hypnotic and psychotherapeutic techniques that activate the imagination allowing access to higher consciousness.

It is our belief that past life, between life and near death studies are among some of the most important on-going research of our time. This work is the leading edge of exploration for our new millennium. Humanity is now seeing the larger picture and reaching toward a vast new level of human realisation. Work involving subconscious memory and regression is, perhaps, one of the greatest endeavours. This therapy will evolve, inevitably, into new careers, technologies, and startling discoveries. The intrinsic value of this particular book, Soul Regression Therapy, is that it provides insight into whom and what we really are. It is the accumulation of research and substantiated soul data.

1. JOHN AND LORNA'S STORY - THEIR SOULS CALLING

LORNA'S STORY

The spiritual quest begins, for most people
as a search for meaning.
Marilyn Ferguson

I didn't consciously set out to become a spiritual regression therapist, far from it. When I was young and first starting out in the work force I knew of no such profession. I believe most people are destined from the beginning of their lives to experience life in such a way that they are drawn to certain professions. I feel that this profession found me.

I have never been able to just coast through life. I have always had a guiding sense of curiosity or quest, searching to understand who I am, what this world is   about, what happens to us when we die and what makes people the way they are.

My incarnation in this life began when I was born in 1950 in a small seaside town on the northwest coast of England called Blackpool. Children born at this time between the years 1946 and 1964 were known as baby boomers. I was a post war baby born just 5 years after WW2 ended and people in Britain were trying to get their lives back to normal after the destruction during the war years and the loss of so many people. Many couples were getting married and the birth rate in England increased to a record high.

My parents Alec and Betty were married in 1945, as newlyweds they lived with my grandparents while they saved to buy a house. One year after I was born my parents bought a new house and moved into a nearby suburb called Bispham. I would say we were a typical English family of the time. My father worked at the local Imperial Chemical plastics factory in Thornton and my mother was a stay at home housewife, as many women were in the 1950's.

My mother was a very sensitive and nervous person. I remember she regularly experienced panic and anxiety attacks when we were out in crowded places, these attacks immobilised her in many ways. She would be confined to her bed for days refusing to go out of the house for months on end. As a child I had no comprehension as to why she was like this, but I understand now that she suffered from a nervous condition called agoraphobia. In the 1960's these attacks were referred to as nervous breakdowns. Many women were given addictive tranquilizers to help them cope with their life. These tranquilizers were known as "mother's little helpers" and were known for numbing down a generation of British housewives in the 1950's and throughout the 60s and 70s. The Rolling Stones wrote a song they titled, "Mother's Little Helper."

> *"Kids are different today, I hear every mother say*
> *Mother needs something today to calm her down. And*
> *though she's not really ill, there's a little yellow pill She*
> *goes running for the shelter of a mother's little helper*
> *And it helps her on her way, gets her through her busy*
> *day" "And if you take more of those you will get an*
> *overdose. No more running for the shelter of a mother's*
> *little helper They just helped you on your way*
> *through your busy dying day."*
> Jagger/Richards

The War Years

The war years were extremely traumatic for the people of England. They were exposed to many horrific things as the Hitler led Germany planned to invade Britain. In September 1940 the Germans began dropping bombs on many cities in Britain. This period was known as "The Blitz." Air raid sirens were a common sound that echoed through the air, warning people that an air raid was coming. After the bombing ceased and the all clear was given many people would return to their homes finding them demolished, during these times hundreds of people were injured and killed.

Before my mother was married she joined the Auxiliary Territorial Service which was known as the ATS. This was the women's branch of the British Army during the Second World War. In December 1941, Parliament passed the National Service Act, which called up unmarried women between the ages of 20 to 30 years to join one of the auxiliary services. When my mother first joined up she was stationed for a few months in the sea side town of Torquay in the South of England.

One day whilst on leave she was at the beach with her friends. They were relaxing in the sun when to their horror a German aircraft flew over the beach and began shooting at the people in the water and on the beach. Terrified my mother scrambled to safety with her friends. I believe because of the trauma of witnessing this horrific and terrifying event it had a detrimental effect on her future mental health. In all probably this caused her to develop the panic attacks and agoraphobic episodes that manifested much later in her life and lead to her being dependant on tranquilizers. As the years went by she became quite paranoid and believed the world was a very unsafe place. My mother's fear caused her to over protect me and as I grew up she tried to keep me at home with her as often as she could.

Growing up

As an only child of a very protective mother my life was very lonely and I kept myself entertained reading books and watching television. I became very curious about the paranormal and quite fascinated with the idea of ghosts and spirits. In order to deepen my understanding ghost stories and science fiction became my favourite form of literature, movies and television choices. There were many of these types of shows and movies on television in the 60's and I regularly enjoyed watching "One Step Beyond" and the "Twilight Zone", which fed my growing interest in paranormal suspense in a different way. Some other favourites of mine were, The Jetson's, Lost in Space, Dr Who, Time Tunnel and Star Trek. These shows triggered my natural curiosity for the paranormal and I wanted to find the answers for myself.

When I was about 13 my introduction to reincarnation and past lives began quite by accident or so I thought. I realise now that nothing is ever an accident. The winter months are long and cold in Blackpool, and sometimes it gets so cold it snows. My dad often worked weekend shifts and when he was working Sundays mum and I watched the Sunday movie together on our small black and white television set. This is where I saw an amazing movie called "Bridey Murphy." The movie was set in America in the early 1950's and was about an amateur hypnotist named Morey Bernstein. He met a 28-year-old American housewife called Mrs Ruth Simmons, she was known later by her actual name, Virginia Tighe. They met at a party where he was demonstrating his hypnosis regression skills. When he hypnotised her, he discovered she was relatively easy to hypnotise and he was able to regress her back to remember her past lives. She was not particularly interested in hypnosis or past lives, but she consented to Bernstein working with her over a period of time, during which she regressed to past life memories where she remembered a life in the 19th-century as an Irish woman named Bridey Murphy. Bernstein recorded all these sessions and kept detailed records which he later published in 1952. The book was called Bridey Murphy, 4 years later in 1956 a movie was released based on the book.

Looking back now I realise whilst living with my parents in

Blackpool, we were in a world of our own, isolated to the concept of reincarnation, what's more, ordinary English people didn't talk about it. My parents were not particularly religious and they had no idea what reincarnation was about. This movie stirred something inside of me it was very different from any other movie or television show I had seen before, I became extremely fascinated and intrigued with the concept of reincarnation and past lives. I now understand that past life regression was becoming more known to the general public in America in the 50's because of this book and movie.

I began asking myself the questions; "Had I lived in times gone by?" "And if I had where did I live and who was I?" I wanted to find out, I wanted to understand the concept deeper. I asked my mother to explain reincarnation to me, but she didn't really understand either. She just replied; "you don't need to know about that." When I asked my dad he just shrugged it off and said he didn't know. I understand now that being inquisitive is a large part of my nature, I am a natural born detective and I want to know the deepest darkest secrets. Back then I had no choice but to put my curiosity to the back of my mind, and I made a mental note that I would find out for myself one day.

Life's Twists and Turns

In 1966 at the age of 15 my life took an unusual turn, my father suddenly fell ill with cancer and passed away in a matter of months. My family of 3 was now 2, it was a sad and lonely time for both my mum and myself and consequently my mother decided that we would immigrate to Australia so she could live close by her sister. I embraced the change and looked upon the move as a great adventure. We settled in Brisbane and I got on with life as most teenagers do.

Becoming more independent I learnt to drive, my first car was an old Austin Lancer that I bought very cheap and it was always breaking down. My boyfriend of that time was a dab hand with mechanics, so he loaned me his red MGA convertible while he worked on fixing up my car. I loved driving his car compared to mine it was amazing. One winter's morning I was driving to work with the top down even though the weather was quite cold, I was wearing a furry hood on my head to keep warm. I was driving slowly in a stream of traffic and just as I approached a stop sign on my left I saw an 8-ton truck approaching the stop sign. The truck was also going slow but it didn't stop at the stop sign, and as I cruised past, the truck rolled into the left side of the MGA I was driving. The sports car was very small compared to this 8-ton truck, and on impact the MGA was pushed into a traffic island on my right.

As the MGA collided with the traffic island it hit a keep left sign which became embedded into the side of the sports car, the impact completely ripped off the driver's door. Everything happened so quickly, but I got such a fright when I looked to my right and saw the road flashing passed where the door used to be. My attention went back to the road ahead as I realised I had been hit by the truck. I instantly put my foot on the break to slow down the car, but to my horror the brakes didn't work because of the impact with the truck. My mind was watching on in the microseconds that followed as if it was watching in slow motion. I was careering down a steep hill, potentially into oncoming traffic. I saw a sharp left hand turn at the bottom of the hill, which if I went that far, the MGA would not have made this sharp turn. The car and I would have either careered into oncoming traffic or crashed over an embankment.

The instant I saw what was happening or could happen, another part of me instantly took over. I automatically looked at the houses on the left side of the road, then I turned the steering wheel sharp right and picked a fence to crash into to stop the car. During the impact of the car colliding into the fence I hit my head on the steering wheel, but other than that I thought I was okay. That was until I tried to get out of the car. As I tried to put my right foot outside of the car and push myself up a lady appeared out of nowhere and told me that I should wait until the ambulance came just to make sure I was okay. I told her I felt fine and I wanted to get out of the car, but she again insisted I stayed where I was. I looked down at my right leg and it felt a little weird and I asked her if there was a problem with my leg, she replied that the ambulance would arrive very soon and they would check to see if I was okay.

The ambulance came and they insisted on lifting me out of the car to check me out. I was told my leg was deeply lacerated and I was rushed to hospital where I had 24 stiches put in my leg. I spent the next 2 weeks in hospital recovering. I was told that I was extremely lucky because the laceration was very close to cutting my sciatic nerve and if that had happened my right leg would have been paralysed. Somehow during the accident, a part of me had reacted in microseconds to a situation that, had I actually had time to think about it, would have been too difficult for me to deal with logically. And yet I had dealt with it, and survived the crash. I had not felt any pain from the car door lacerating my leg when it was torn off by the traffic sign. It was as if presented with a situation that required more than my minds usual ability to respond, my mind had worked out what to do to stay safe. How had I done this?

At the time I hadn't given much thought to how I had survived, I was just relieved to have come out of the situation alive, even though I had a deep laceration to my leg. I realize now that the real answer to that question is much more profound and I had to experience many changes in my life to understand the answer. My higher mind or my Soul mind was the part of me that took over from my logic mind and steered the car to safety that day. It wasn't my time to leave and my Soul made sure of this.

I have since researched my astrological natal chart which revealed I had the potential to be involved in a freak car accident at some point in my life. To explain this simply I have the planet Mars sitting in my first house, the first house in astrology is commonly referred to as the house of Self. I have Mars trine Uranus in my natal chart, and this aspect indicates freak accidents with cars, explosives, guns, electricity and lightning. Mars also represents scars. There are many types of accident configurations and most of them involve Mars. John F. Kennedy, Rajiv Gandhi, Versace and Princess Diana were born with a Mars-Uranus aspect and they all died from freak accidents. I thought I was very lucky, but now know it wasn't luck at all it was the synchronicity of my higher mind at work.

I eventually married, and my daughter was born in 1973, you could say I was a typical wife of the 70's in Australia. My life followed along its main stream path for many years until, one day whilst recovering from a horse riding accident I went to a garage sale and as I rummaged through a large box I came across a book written by the actress Shirley MacLaine titled "Out on a Limb". I had always admired her, having seen many of her movies on television, not knowing at the time she was an author as well as an actress. Out on a Limb was an autobiography describing Shirley's personal journey through New Age spirituality, in this book she discussed such topics as reincarnation, meditation, mediumship and unidentified flying objects. I found the book to be really fascinating, the subjects she covered opened my mind to many possibilities, so much so I just couldn't put it down, devouring it from cover to cover in no time at all. My interest in reincarnation was once again awakened and I also became interested in psychics and meditation.

Around this time, I came across some books by Edgar Cayce, he is well known as the sleeping prophet. Cayce is probably the most documented psychic of the 20th century, with more than 40 years of work documented during his adult life. Cayce had the ability to take himself into an unconscious state, which we now know to be self-hypnosis. While he was in this state he was able to access what he called the Akashic records, give accurate psychic readings, diagnose illnesses and reveal lives lived in the past and also predict the future. The more I read the more I wanted to know.

Recovering from the fall off my horse I got very bored lying around and felt really down. One day while I was at my local doctors, I noticed a sign on the waiting room wall advertising meditation classes. It described how meditation can help to relieve stress and bring about relaxation. Remembering what I had read in MacLaines' and Cayces' books about meditation I decided to check it out. The meditation teacher was called Stella, she was a lovely older woman in her 60s and taught privately 1 on 1 at her home. Her small house fascinated me, it was filled with crystals, Buddha statues and there was a soft sound of wind chimes coming in through the window. The air was filled with the sweet fragrance of incense. Stella was very patient with me as she explained the principals of meditation.

At first I found trying to still my mind to be very difficult, Stella gave me a tape to play at home which she said would help. I only visited her couple of times, but I listened to the tape daily as well as reading my books and found I was able to still my mind and meditate quite well after a few weeks. I believe meditation helped me to connect to a higher source that is within us all and this connection got me through one of the most difficult times in my life, and I began to re-connect to my soul essence.

Health Issues

After experiencing many years of chronic back pain from the horse fall I eventually decided to undergo spinal surgery. I didn't make this decision lightly, I had tried many alternative therapies over the years with no results and I was feeling depressed at the thought of spending the rest of my life restricted with chronic pain. Sitting there on the edge of my hospital bed barely moments before they took me to the operating theatre to have a double spinal fusion I made a decision, that decision was to be another major turning point in my life. I decided that if this surgery was successful then I would do my upmost best to change my life completely. Deep down I had been very unhappy for many years.

The surgery was very successful, during the 4-hour operation the neurosurgeon fused 2 vertebras in my low back together with wire and a steel plate. After a 2 week stay in hospital I was finally allowed to go home, at this point I was feeling more positive about my future than I had felt for years. The medical team were very pleased with the progress I had made in such a short time and the fusion stabilised my spine and the pain was reduced considerably. Around this time, I began reading a New Age magazine called the Silver Cord. I was keen to read as much as I could about psychic and spiritual phenomena. As I began to contemplate life and the world even deeper, I became more conscious of my inner self. This lead me to feel there was something missing in my life and as I recovered from the surgery and the months went by my desire to find out what was missing became even stronger.

In an attempt to understand myself and my future on a deeper level I went to see a psychic reader. He asked for a piece of jewellery and I gave him a signet ring, which he held tightly in the palm of his hand. He began to tell me things about my present life and future that really surprised me. He confirmed how unhappy I was with my life and my relationship with my husband but he said not to worry because my life would change very soon. He also told me there was someone else coming into my life and this person was waiting for me, and this would be a happy relationship. I was really shocked with this news, but he was spot on with how I felt and I wondered if the future would turn out as he said. I know now that the psychic was doing a psychometry reading. Psychometry is the ability to gain impressions from objects by holding or touching them. This ability allows the psychic to sense an object's history or obtain information about the person who owned the item and is sometimes referred to as 'sensing with the fingers'.

The Past Returns

About a week before my 39th birthday I received a phone call that was to change my life and hurl me into a totally new direction. This call was from my ex finance Brian inviting me to attend a reunion. He was organising a party for some friends from the 60's and wanted to know if I could go. As it turned out I didn't go, but we did meet up for a coffee a few weeks later. This meeting was the beginning of a huge change in my life, we realised we wanted to be together again. Neither of us were happy with our lives and we realised that we still had strong feelings for each other. We decided to reunite and as this became a reality I realised the psychic's prediction had come true.

Life was going really well for us, and I had an uneasy feeling this might be too good to be true. My feeling was right on, because a few months later Brian noticed a lump on his stomach, just under his belly button, it was the size of a 20 cent piece, and was very sore to touch. One day he was in the car putting his seat belt on when the belt slipped and hit the lump, causing him to be in agony. I explained this wasn't right, it shouldn't hurt like that and he needed go to the doctors immediately to get it checked out.

After much encouraging he finally went along to the doctor who was extremely concerned and referred him to a see a specialist. The specialist took some tests and the results came back a week later with the grim diagnosis that he had a high level of malignant melanoma cancer. The specialist explained he could have surgery to remove the tumour, this may slow down the cancer, but the survival rate was low. As you can imagine we were both devastated with this news and it felt like our world was falling apart. After many months battling melanoma cancer Brian passed away at our home in the early morning of 20th July, 1996. His death left a gaping hole in my heart and my life, I felt like my life was a living nightmare, and I had no idea what I would do now he was gone. We had only been back together for 3 years when he died. We had bought a new house together and made so many plans for our future as a couple. We had become engaged with plans to get married, we were trying to catch up for the time we had lost over the years.

The strange thing was, while I was waiting to have my spinal surgery I had begun to think of Brian a lot, I wondered where he was and how his life had turned out. I even thought he might be dead, maybe from cancer. One day I flipped through the local phone book and found his name and address. I was very tempted to call him, but I didn't know what to say after so many years. He must have picked up telepathically on my thoughts or maybe I picked up on his, because he called me out of the blue only a year later regarding the reunion, and said he had been thinking about me on and off for over a year and wondered where I was, and what I was doing.

When my initial grief and shock I felt over Brian's passing began to subside, I found myself becoming overwhelmed by a whole new set of feelings of confusion and bewilderment. I felt as if I had been caught totally unaware, not so much by his death but by the very fact that death existed at all. I had lost my Nana and Father many years before but nothing had prepared me for this awful confrontation with reality. I understand now as a therapist that everyone probably experiences their first real confrontation with death much the same way I did, but our reactions to this personal event are always individual. My reaction eventually subsided and was replaced by a desperate need to understand death itself, if such a thing was possible. Brian's death was the catalyst that propelled me on a spiritual journey of self-discovery. I began my quest by reading everything I could get my hands on relating to the subject of death, reincarnation and the afterlife that seemed to hold any chance of unravelling this most ancient of all mysteries.

I have learnt that everyone comes to an emotional crisis point in their life, often between the age of 35 to 45. This crisis can be triggered by a relationship break up, the loss of a job, a physical illness or the death of a loved one. This crisis point is where life becomes really difficult and depression or anxiety often sets in. Looking back, I experienced a physical illness, major surgery, a relationship breakdown and the loss of a loved one all in a 3-year time frame. These types of crisis often propel people to step onto a journey of self-discovery and to search for the meaning of life as I did. A metaphor for this emotional struggle is the mythological bird the phoenix. The phoenix is a bird that obtains new life by rising from the ashes of its predecessor. The meaning is, surrendering to a time of great difficulty, while allowing the pain to break you open to be reborn stronger and wiser. We all have a choice as to how we deal with a crisis, some people numb down their pain with drugs, alcohol and antidepressants or they develop addictions to food, gambling, etc. As a therapist I have seen a lot of clients over the years who have taken the negative paths to avoid their feelings, I chose to go down the path of the phoenix, to look within myself, as well as researching death and the afterlife in order to heal.

My spiritual quest eventually led me to travel extensively through America and to live in California for 9 months. While I was there I had the time and opportunity to research metaphysics, the paranormal, reincarnation and the between life realms in great depth. On my return to Brisbane I continued my metaphysical studies and was a member of a magical group for some years. This was where I learnt many spiritual modalities including astrology, magick and the tarot. I also experienced my first past life regression and a group member gave me a copy of the book "Many Lives Many Masters" written by American Psychiatrist Dr Brian Weiss. This book further ignited my interest in past lives, which eventually led me to become a Clinical Hypnotherapist specialising in Past Life Regression, Life Between Lives Hypnotherapy and co-creating Soul Regression Therapy.

JOHN'S STORY

Some changes look negative but you will soon realise
that space is being created in your life for something
new to emerge.

Eckhart Tolle

So a little bit about me. I incarnated into this existence in Wellington New Zealand,1956. In total I spent 32 years living in Wellington before moving around the country several times finally leaving New Zealand to reside permanently in Australia in 2004. Like Lorna I never imagined that I would one day become a hypnotherapist and be involved in such a fantastic industry let alone co create our own regression modality Soul Regression Therapy.

My Spiritual interests began at around the age of 17 after meeting an older man named Pete who at the time was in his mid-60s, though he appeared to most a lot younger. One afternoon I called into his house and disturbed him whilst he lay relaxing in the sun. He told me he had been meditating and astral traveling. Well this was completely new to me so naturally being inquisitive I asked him to explain more which he did. He explained that he often drifted out of his earthly body and transcended into another level of existence, a realm where spirits of those who have passed over resided. He often spoke to them and he also told me he could also observe earth bound spirits below who he described as being those that had committed heinous crimes and their punishment was to remain bound to the earth plane whilst having to see the free spirits floating above them. These earthbound spirits would try to entice him to come down to them, but he said that was their way of trying to attach to him as an entity.

These conversations I had with Pete totally changed my concept of things on a spiritual level. I had been raised by my parents, Derek and Wyn in a fairly non-religious way, even though as a child they encouraged me to go to the local Sunday schools, main stream religion never sat comfortably with me.

Looking back now my mother was a bit of a closet psychic, she was always quite superstitious, reading horoscopes, teacups, and always on the lookout for a four leaf clover on her walks to and from the bus. Her intuitive ability was uncanny and many a time after assessing my friends I would find out later she was spot on, usually accompanied with an I told you so from mum.

My first actual encounter with spirit occurred when I was 24, at the time I was living in a rented a house with a group of friends. One evening after going to bed early, I awoke again about an hour after my head had hit the pillow to see a mist covering the wall in front of me. Feeling half-awake observing this strange scene in front of the bed, I quickly became more alert as a form emerged from the mist and drifted up alongside the side of the bed I was sleeping on. As the form drew closer I recognised it as the torso of a person which then became clearer as if it was refocusing its energy to help assist me to see it. It was at that moment I recognised the face though very skeletal of a close family friend named Johnny. Johnny was currently staying in a hospice under palliative care whilst in the final stages of cancer. I said "is that you Johnny" to which the spirit form replied, "yes I've just come to say goodbye", all I could manage to say was "goodbye then Johnny" as I was feeling really stunned by what was happening before me. The spirit of Johnny then drifted back towards the mist covered wall and as his spirit approached, the mist parted and revealed to me a mountainous scene. Johnny continued drifting in to this scene then he floated down onto a mountain top and became a whole person again. He was standing alongside a large but plain marble alter and beside him stood a Christ like figure. They both looked at me and then the mist closed over and disappeared. I noted the time on my bedside clock which read 9.30pm.

The next morning, I phoned my mother to relate what had happened, as soon as she answered I said to her "before you tell me anything Johnny passed away last night at approximately 9.30pm" her voice hesitated slightly and then she said "how do you know that". I then told her that he had visited me to say goodbye. She then related to me that she and my father were at his bedside as he passed at 9.25pm and that she was holding his hand as he departed. From that moment on I never doubted the existence of spirit or the continuation of life after death.

I began reading more and more books, mainly self-help but including some with a more spiritual aspect. One day a friend suggested going to an Indian aura healer they had seen. I decided on the day of my appointment to remain fairly tight lipped about myself so as not to give anything away and taint the session. I was shown into the front room of the house and instructed to lie on a large sofa and the healer began passing his hands through my auric fields and as he did so, he began relating to me my health problems and also he viewed into my past lives. After the healing session had finished he told me that my house where I was living was in need of clearing. I immediately became weary thinking he was about to suggest that he come and clear it for a fee but instead he told me that I was spiritually strong and could easily do it myself. So following his instructions I cleansed my home and have done similar wherever I have lived. Not long after this experience I learnt Transcendental Meditation from a T.M organisation in Wellington and learned to meditate deeply. I also started to practice automatic writing, a skill I came to call upon to help make decisions in my life. I found that whatever I connected to in trance whilst writing would often chastise me, and give me direction that in hindsight would have saved me some emotionally painful times had I followed the advice given. However, I have learnt to have no regrets in life as it's all a predestined karmic plan and that if I choose one way and it's wrong then karma will intervene and have its way, my lesson will be learnt albeit harder than originally planned and life will continue along its prechosen course.

In 2004 I made some serious life choices and left New Zealand for Australia, somehow I knew I would never permanently return. Since a visit to Brisbane in the early 90s I had felt this part of the world held a strong connection in my heart and that one day I must come here to live. So on the 28th June 2004 I arrived. Some 6 months later I met my wife Lorna and as the years have flown by we have had so many wonderful and interesting times together. Interestingly during the time, I had previously visited Brisbane, I stayed only a few streets away from where Lorna lived at the time, we may have even passed each other in the street never realising we were destined to one-day meet. Not long after Lorna and I met I had an incident involving my lower back which I have had ongoing problems on and off with since 1980 along with several operations. As a result of the repeated injuries and surgery I was left with ongoing chronic pain and having to sporadically take pain medication to ease the pain. On this occasion my back had spasmed whilst bending over to straighten a lawn sprinkler hose. I was stuck in a semi bent forward lopsided position. The pain was excruciating and even though I had sought medical care the pain hadn't eased. In fact, I was advised I may need further surgery. I phoned Lorna who said to me why don't we try a session of hypnosis and see if it helps at all. I had nothing to lose so I found myself being knowingly hypnotised for the first time. After the session finished which felt as if 5 minutes had elapsed instead of the actual hour it took, I arose from the recliner chair and within 10 minutes I was walking without any pain whatsoever and have never suffered chronic pain again to the debilitating extent I had in the past. This amazing turn around inspired my interest in hypnosis and the pursuit of a new career. I knew hypnotherapy worked and that I could possibly help many others.

As of this present time I have now been involved in hypnotherapy for 10 years and in that time have witnessed some amazing results in the use of hypnosis both in my own clients and also in the work of other professionals. Lorna and myself have undertaken many hours of training in various hypnotic modalities including those of regression to both past life and between lives. We have now bought together all of our knowledge and life skills to co-create Soul Regression Therapy which we train throughout Australia. It's fantastic to see the students we train beginning to grow as therapists and have their own successful practices. I have a feeling that this is just the beginning of a whole new chapter in my life accompanied by my lovely wife Lorna. I have no plans to retire as I view retirement as re – tiring oneself and who wants to spend their best years feeling tired. John.

2. ORIGINS OF PAST LIFE AND SPIRITUAL REGRESSION

Our birth is but a sleep and a forgetting...The soul that rises with us, our life star, has had elsewhere its setting and cometh from afar. William Wordsworth

The belief in past lives, reincarnation and the afterlife is a very ancient concept, although the current hypnotic regression methods of exploring this belief are in historic terms very recent. The theory of reincarnation was originally recorded in the Bible, in both the Old and New Testaments. In A.D. 325 the Roman emperor Constantine the Great, and his mother Helena, deleted some of these references. Then later the proper interpretations were removed during an Ecumenical Council meeting of the Catholic Church in Constantinople sometime around 553 A.D, called the Council of Nicaea. It is believed by some that the Council members voted to take those teachings from the Bible in order for the Church to have control over the people. And because the church wanted to control the people, they told their followers that the Christian religion, priests and the church were the only ones who had the answers and through them was the only way to reach God. This is an extremely dogmatic view, most people today have no idea that reincarnation was originally a belief of Christianity or that reincarnation was effectively erased from the minds of the general public. In the western world the concept of reincarnation was

18

driven underground, living on only in the secret worlds of mystics, occultists and spiritualists until in the late 19th century mysticism and spiritualism became the fashion.

One of the most influential people to change these views was Madame Blavatsky, she established the Theosophical Society, in New York in 1875. Theosophy brought the influence of eastern spiritual beliefs to the west, and was responsible for introducing the idea of reincarnation to the western world.

Also at this time popular awareness of the idea of reincarnation was boosted by magical societies such as The Golden Dawn and the Rosicrucians and a man named Allan Kardec who released his inspirational book called, "The Book of the Spirits" (1857). Kardec had a brush with past lives and wrote in his book, how "spirits" spoke to him through mesmerized patients regarding reincarnation and karma.

As a therapy, past life regression has been developed since the early 1950's by psychiatrists, psychologists, psychotherapists and mediums. One of the first people to use regression as a therapy was a psychologist called Dr Denys Kelsey. Kelsey wrote a book, "Many Lifetimes" this book focuses more on the therapeutic aspect of the technique of past life regression than on case studies. The book was co-authored with his wife Joan Grant who was a well know psychic medium, in the book she explained how she remembered her own and others peoples past lives.

There have been many pioneers in the field of past life regression. One of the more well-known and leading advocates is Dr Brian Weiss, a graduate of Columbia University and Yale Medical School and a Chairman Emeritus of Psychiatry at the Mount Sinai Medical Centre in Miami. His research includes reincarnation, past life regression and survival of the human soul after death. Dr Weiss is well known to the public for his first book "Many Lives Many Masters", released in 1988. This book is about a patient he treated named Catherine who began remembering her past life experiences while in hypnosis. Dr Weiss believes that many present-life phobias and ailments are rooted in past-life experiences.

Australian psychologist Peter Ramster, developed an interest in reincarnation and has written books on this subject. He also created a television documentary in 1983 called "The Reincarnation Experiments" this followed Ramster regressing his clients and then travelling across the world with them to their past life location. He found amazing evidence that reconnected to them to their past lives.

Dolores Cannon is another pioneer in the development and acceptance of the healing powers of remembering past lives. She has been working in this field for over 50 years and written over 17 books on this subject which contain hundreds of fascinating case studies of clients who remember their past lives not only on earth but on other planets.

3. PIONEERS DISCOVER THE BETWEEN LIFE REALMS

Many of the past life regression pioneers expanded their belief systems by investigating what happens in the realm between lives. They came across this realm by accident when clients described a place where they would go between lifetimes. This place known as the spiritual plane is where all souls go to plan and prepare for the next life or incarnation. In this realm the soul rests, healing from a difficult or traumatic life just lived then reconnecting with spirit friends and also meeting and learning from spiritual advisors. This time between lives allows the soul to consider karmic destiny and make choices that will best fulfil that destiny. The belief that all souls ascend to a spirit place or realms between physical lives, is well recorded in the "Tibetan Book of the Dead."

Probably the first pioneer and person to research and document modern hypnotic regression to the afterlife was Canadian Psychiatrist Dr Joel Whitton. He collaborated with author and journalist Joe Fisher who also had a deep interest in spirituality and metaphysics. Together they wrote and published the first book on the subject of between life regression in 1986 titled, "Life Between Life, Scientific Explorations into the Void Separating One Incarnation from the Next." This book contains many case studies from Dr Whitton's clients and their experiences while in hypnotic regression. The book also discusses what occurs between lives and Dr Whitton calls this state of existence between lives "metaconsciousness". He describes this as, "a wondrous state that occurs after death, the threshold of consciousness experienced that separates one incarnation from another." John found a copy of this amazing book on the internet and when it arrived we were surprised to find it was signed by the late Joe Fisher.

Another pioneer and author of this subject is Dr Michael Newton. He researched the afterlife through hypnotic regression with his clients over 40 years. He documented his findings in his first book, "Journey of Souls," (1996) and has since published other books on this subject which have popularised Life Between Lives as a therapy. Dr Newton co-created a certification training program called Life –Between- Lives Hypnotherapy. I was part of the first group of students to be trained in Life Between Lives Hypnotherapy in Sydney, Australia and John travelled down to be part of one of the Melbourne courses a few years later. I was also a training assistant at this course in Melbourne.

Alan and Dee Chips, both Master Hypnotherapists and executive directors of the National Association of Transpersonal Hypnotherapists in USA were also the co-creators of the original Life-Between-Lives certification program with Dr Newton. Alan Chips has written a number of books on this subject, sadly Alan passed away a few years ago. Dee Chips has carried on with the work and continues to teach a Life Between Lives certification training program in the USA.

Andy Tomlinson is another pioneer in the between lives movement, Andy is a regression therapist from the UK, international trainer and author in this field. He has written many books on the subject of past life regression and the afterlife. I was fortunate to meet Andy and spend some time with him when he was in Brisbane a few years ago. He was in Australia teaching a series of spiritual workshops and John and I enrolled in his 3-day Entity Releasement Workshop. Being from England myself I was quite curious to know where he was born and had lived in the UK, but I wasn't prepared for what he told me. As it turned out he was born in the very same town, Blackpool and the synchronicities didn't stop there. He had lived very close to where I had lived and we had both attended the same high school at the same time, although he was a year older and a year ahead of me our paths would have crossed at some stage. We could never have imagined back then when we were teenagers that we would both be a part of this amazing work that can help so many people.

Dolores Cannon discovered the between life state through her clients. She began her work with her husband back in the early 60's and has written many books about past lives and also a book about the afterlife titled "Between Death and Life." Dolores travelled extensively around the world speaking at spiritual conferences and teaching her own method of past life regression therapy named "Quantum Healing Hypnosis." Sadly, Dolores passed away in October 2014, but her amazing work and the legacy she has left will live on through her daughter Julia Cannon who continues to teach Quantum Healing Hypnosis process. I was very fortunate to have met and trained personally with the lovely Dolores, having done both her courses and I'm listed as one of her advanced QHH practitioners on her web site.

Deep Memory Process (DMP), founded by Roger Woolger is another form of therapy that helps the client to access the afterlife or Bardo realms to heal complexes. DMP has been described as a practical and highly effective therapy of the soul. This combines active imagination (Jung), bodywork (Reich) and psychodrama (Moreno) with shamanic/spirit journeying and integration between lifetimes derived from the Buddhist Bardo wisdom of "The Tibetan Book of the Dead." Deep Memory Process has been recognised as a major contribution to transpersonal psychotherapy. Roger Woolger also passed away a few years ago, but his work lives on through his head trainer Patricia Walsh. John and myself both travelled to Melbourne a few years ago where we took part in an intensive 5-day Deep Memory Process course that was facilitated by Patricia Walsh.

4. HOW WE REMEMBER THE PAST

Hypnotic regression therapy is generally a standard part of the therapeutical training that is taught to students who study to become clinical hypnotherapists. Hypnotic regression therapy differs from many other forms of therapy in that it deals with the subconscious mind rather the conscious mind.

The Conscious Mind

The conscious mind uses only approx. 10 to 18% of the brains capacity and is the part associated with the waking state. This is the part that is responsible for logical thinking, analysing, will power, and contains the short term memory. Our conscious mind is very limited and seems only able to keep track of 7 bits of information at one time. As adults this part of the mind has the power to decide and filter what information will enter into the subconscious mind. As children it is wide open and like a sponge, absorbing all information.

Your conscious mind also has the power to reprogram your subconscious mind, mainly through repetition. For instance, can you remember the first time you learnt to drive a car, when you had to consciously think of which peddle to press and which gear to shift. As a driver you no longer have to consciously think of these actions now they have become automatic, i.e. you are able to do it subconsciously. Through repetition, you have programmed your subconscious mind and created a habit and once a habit is in your subconscious, it becomes automatic. While it's true for driving a car, it is also true for achieving success in life.

The Subconscious or Unconscious Mind

The subconscious mind is approx. 90% of your mind. This part of your mind is like a computer, but is far superior to any computer yet created and plays many different roles in your life.

The subconscious mind is concerned with: Dreaming, reflecting, meditating, sleeping, emotions, imagination, self-preservation mechanism, permanent memory, habits, addictions, fears and trauma. This inner part of your mind is made up of lots of programs like on a computer. These programs communicate to your outer logic mind through your thoughts and feelings. Once a program is installed in your computer mind it just runs automatically unless you decide you no longer need it and then you can uninstall or delete it if you know how, most people don't know how. An example of a negative program running in your subconscious mind is the habit of smoking.

The subconscious mind is far greater than we can imagine, and is often referred to as the unconscious or internal mind because there is an internal part to the subconscious mind that runs on autopilot and governs the bodily functions, autonomic nervous system, immune system, and automatically controls the internal organs: how you breathe, sends oxygen to your blood cells, the ability to walk without using the conscious mind.

Forgotten Memories

The concept that the brain holds forgotten memories was documented by Karl Pribram. He researched this by working with a woman who had a hole in her skull and her brain could be safely stimulated with a probe. One day when he stimulated a neurological pathway, she had vivid memories of an early childhood event around age 2 that she had forgotten. This experiment proved that memories are forgotten by the conscious mind but are stored neurologically in the brain where they may still affect us.

The subconscious mind is a complex system with many programs running. This is where all our long term memories are stored, which include childhood, womb and past life memories. If you imagine your subconscious mind is like a computer and in it are stored all your past lives, like corrupted programs that interfere with how the computer functions. Some of these programs are close to the surface and some are buried very deeply. This computer runs your body and how you feel and often these corrupted programs can cause negative unwanted feelings to emerge from a soul level that don't make much sense to the logic conscious mind. Some of the problems that may emerge from a soul level could be depression, fears, compulsions, guilt, anger, resentment, shame. The philosopher George Santayana said that, "Those who cannot remember the past are condemned to repeat it". Through regression we can access old traumatic memories and heal them to free ourselves from the controlling power of our past lives.

When I set out to become a hypnotic regression therapist I was searching for evidence of the survival of the soul after death. I now know that reincarnation is real, I know it's real because I have facilitated thousands of past life regression sessions with my clients. I have been privileged to have witnessed firsthand their amazing experiences as they described the details of their womb experiences as well as past lives and death experiences.

5. LORNA'S FIRST PAST LIFE REGRESSION CLIENT

A SEARCH FOR HAPPINESS

*Happiness cannot be travelled to, owned, earned, worn
or consumed. Happiness is the spiritual experience of
living every minute with love, grace, and gratitude*
Denis Waitley

Dianne and I had been friends for many years and when I asked her if she would be my first volunteer to practise a past life regression on she kindly said yes. I felt very excited at the possibility of discovering her past life memories and I felt I was well prepared. I had written out a past life regression script from a book I was reading. I had never hypnotised Dianne before, and had no idea how this session would go, or even if I could hypnotise her at all, but I felt confident. As she lay down on the couch in her lounge room I began the hypnotic induction and she quickly and easily drifted into a very deep hypnotic state. Once she was nicely relaxed I began to guide her back in time, back through her memory to remember a time before her current life and to tell me when she was there and where she was. She began speaking in a very soft voice;

> D: I'm in a garden, standing at a big clothes line, there are children at my feet, and I'm hanging out the washing

and laughing. My daughter has a pram with a doll and she is playing. I can see my husband on the back stairs, he is smiling. He has a beard and a pipe; he has happy eyes and brown hair. He looks a bit scraggly and his name is Tom.

I was really surprised as she began to describe the details and I eagerly asked her questions.

L: *Can you tell me more about this, how do you look?*

D: I'm wearing a dress with an apron and I have long blonde hair tied up in a bun. I'm about 27 and my name is Lyn. I only have 1 child, a daughter called Chrissie. The other children are from the neighbours. The house where I live is wooden, painted white and there are verandas all around. It's very big and there are 7 steps leading up to the house. The windows have lace curtains and it's breezy today and they are blowing in the wind.

L: *Can you tell me more about Tom?*

D: Tom works away, he goes away for months at a time. He is a drover and I miss him when he's away, it's always happy when he's back, everyone is happy.

L: *Where is this place where you live?*

D: This is New South Wales, in Australia and we live in the country in a little village and there are other houses. Baree is the name of this place. My family is a long way away in Victoria and I don't see them very much. I came here with Tom, he was from Victoria and we moved for his work and he goes away for months on end.

After this session I did some research and found that Baree is an outlying district of Mount Morgan located near Rockhampton in Queensland. It's interesting to note that on 6 June 1859 Queen Victoria signed Letters to form the colony of Queensland. And on 10th December 1859 Queensland was formally separated from New South Wales to become an independent state of Australia. I moved Jenny forward in time so that we could find out more about her life as Lyn...and we moved to a turning point in her life;

L: *Where are you now, I asked curiously?*

D: I'm 54 and I have hurt my left hip, I'm lying in bed... it's made it really hard. Tom has died and I am back in Victoria with my family helping my brother and his wife with their family. Tom was in a fire, he was away working and he was caught in a bush fire, he never came back. It was hard, a lot of waiting I didn't find out for a long time.

I asked her if Tom reminded her of anyone in her current life and she said he reminded her of her husband in her current life as Dianne. When the person is in a deep hypnotic state and fully engaged in the details of a regression they are directly connected to their subconscious mind. They can access far memories when in this state, but there is usually a part of their mind that is aware of the present time. This is why they are able to recognise people in the past life. Quite often they recognise the soul essence of the person and realise the same soul has reincarnated with them in their current life but in a different body. We often reincarnate with the same souls and these souls are generally members of our soul family.

L: *Is there anyone with you?*

D: Yes, Chrissie is with me and she is in her 30's now. I hurt my hip and it's getting worse, I'm struggling to walk with it now, I will have to go into town to the doctor. I was hoping it will heal itself, but it's getting worse. The town is Bendigo and we have to take the horses, I usually ride a horse, but this time I will have to ride in the cart. It takes hours to get there and it's very hot.

D: My brother works on the farm and grows our food. He has lots of children and there's no money. He's out in the fields and we look after the children. He is my son in my current life and Chrissie is my step daughter in my current life.

I moved her forward again in this life.

D: I'm now at my brother's funeral... he was trodden on by the horses, his name was Simon. I'm 62 now and his wife Matilda is very upset. The children are grown and they are trying to help her. I know it won't be long now until I am ready to go. Life's hard and tough, I feel like I'm tough now. We will have to work the fields ourselves now, it's very hard. Chrissie is still with me, she never left.

I now moved her to the end of this life, to her death.

D: I'm 63...I'm lying in the dirt resting. I was trying to get to Chrissie she is in town and I ran out of water and my hip is sore. I'm walking to town because she took the last horse. Matilda needed help, she is very sick and I wanted to catch up with her before she got to town. The boys don't know what to do, I shouldn't have left her. I'm hoping she will come back soon and find me. I had 2 bags of water, but I didn't check them and 1 was half empty... I lay there a very long time and it's ok now Chrissie never came back.

As Dianna left her body she said she felt ready to leave... she described her death as a peaceful feeling... It's very familiar... I'm moving away very slow. As she reflected on the life she had just lived she said.

D: Life got hard and in the way... I didn't get as close to Matilda and the children as I would have liked... we were together but I still didn't get to know her, life was hard for everybody. We didn't give each other what we really needed, to show each other we were there for each other. I think we all knew but the closeness wasn't there because we were so busy surviving.

L: *What's happening now?*

D: I'm in a bubble and it's just me standing in a bubble of light, bright light. There are fleeting lights around, other beings around in their own bubbles. They are not taking any notice of me, just doing their own thing as I'm slowly floating around.

As she connected to her higher self I asked her to reflect on the life just lived as Lyn and to let me know why she was shown that life.

D: I was shown that life so that Dianna won't make her life as hard in the future, although it made my soul stronger this is not what life is about. Hardness does not lead to happiness. To be there for others and to show them love. Not to always focus on the hardships to find the light.

She went on to explain.

D: Dianna tends to focus on the positives now but tends to put her value in hard work. She thinks that if she works hard it will lead to happiness. But you need to be happy; the work just pushes aside the time for happiness. Jenny needs to balance, to find the balance, she tries but the happiness will be valued more than the hard work. Her main lesson here is to learn to let go. She is learning that all the obstacles that get put in the way are insignificant if you let them flow, they are never as big as you make them out to be. Life is about finding happiness and it's always there if you push the obstacles aside and look for the light, it's always there. She worries too much about what might be. She needs to appreciate what is more. She worries too much about the future and different scenarios that may or may not happen. But if it's not happening now don't focus on it and bring it to life. Just be happy with where you are now and happiness will bring more happiness.

L: *Is this a theme or pattern over more lives?*

D: Yes a lot of lives, 2 other lives where she has been searching for happiness when it was already there. In the life as Lyn the happiness was there, but she was too busy worrying to enjoy the people and the happiness. One other life was lived in Europe as a man, his name was Beauregard and he was wealthy and extremely arrogant, he thought he had all the answers. He wore a blue suit, and he thought it was important how others perceived him... it was all about how he was seen by others. He was very cocky and he died when he was hit by a tram as a young man.

L: *What have you learned from that life as Beauregard?*

D: What matters most is how you see yourself, not how

others see you. He thought everybody loved him and he only cared about what people thought about him... but he was a really ugly person on the inside. He should have taken more care about who he wanted to be and about himself rather than what he thought everybody else wanted him to be. He wasn't happy; he thought he would find happiness through the eyes of others and what they thought. If they all liked him then he would be happy. He wanted to impress people but he didn't do a very good job.

L: *Who were you in the other life?*

D: The other life was a female life, her name was Lynette and she flirted with everyone. She was always partying, drinking and laughing, but it was a fake laugh. She had many, many lovers and she moved from one person to the next very quickly. She thought she was happy but she wasn't and she died in a fire when she was quite young.

L: *Can you see a thread or pattern that runs through these lives?*

D: Yes...she is trying to find happiness and the perception of happiness. It seems that in the lives they are searching and searching for happiness in some way. But you don't need to search it's right there... just grab it and be happy.

L: *What does Dianna need to do to find happiness in her current life?*

D: She just needs to stop every now and then. She knows the happiness is there but she worries that if she doesn't keep working hard that it will go... but it won't go. She is still trying to prove herself to everyone else... but she doesn't need to, it's all within herself. She is trying to prove that she is worth being with, by working so hard and she thinks this will lead her to being happy. But it has the opposite effect... working hard pushes her family away if anything. It's about pride as well, once again it's how other people perceive what she does. She doesn't want to be seen as lazy or not contributing to the family.

A few weeks after her session Dianna contacted me by email and this is what she had to say about her session.

The past life regression session I had with Lorna really opened my eyes, I had never been hypnotised before, but I trusted Lorna totally and knew that whatever happened, whatever I told her, was ok. I surprised myself as I answered her questions (with thoughts of, where is this coming from, you can't just say whatever comes into your head) but I did and the story unfolded. I was happy to find that I had spent another life with my current family and felt like this is something I already knew, but the confirmation was nice. The session brought up issues that I was mildly aware of, but were having a big impact on my current life - to bring these issues to the surface was something I really needed to happen to be able to move past them or at least begin working on them. - The emotions I felt during the session also surprised me, with the 'current me' piping in occasionally with 'what are you crying for???', when the session ended, I felt so much better, I now had an awareness of why I react the way I do in my current life and how to work on changing those reactions for the better.

6. LORNA'S INTEREST DEEPENS

Dianna's session was amazing and I knew deep down she wasn't making it up by the way she described the what was going on, the emotions she expressed and how her facial expressions changed as she described the details of her past life.. She was really living the experience; it was as if she was really in the past. Her voice was charged with emotion as she described the details of her past life and how she felt. At that moment I realised reincarnation must be real because I knew she wasn't making this up. After this session my interest deepened even further and I decided I would spend more time researching this fascinating subject.

I had taken a course in basic hypnosis and discovered I could hypnotise people quite easily. I began practising my hypnotic skills on a few more of my friends who wanted to stop smoking. I was successful in getting them into a hypnotic state but I had limited success helping them to make changes. I began to realised that if I wanted to make clinical hypnotherapy a career I really needed to take some further training. I searched the local phone book for hypnotherapy training and I found a reputable college on the Gold Coast. I enrolled in the Diploma course and I proudly graduated as a fully qualified Clinical Hypnotherapist on the 25th September 2004.

I learnt so much from this course and my confidence increased. I decided I would focus on building my hypnotherapy practice and specialise in past life regression. I took out a small advert in a local magazine promoting my clinical services and I advertised past life regression sessions in a new age magazine. I was given an old recliner chair and I turned my spare room into a hypnotherapy clinic. As the months progressed I began to see a steady stream of clients whom I learnt a lot from.

My clinical hypnotherapy business was doing well, but I wanted to learn more about past life regression. And in 2007 I went down to Sydney and was part of a 3-day course in past life regression held by the Holistic Healing Centre of New York. The head trainer Paul Aruand came over from New York to teach this course. I returned to Sydney in 2008 and was part of the first Life Between Lives certificate training course held in Australia by The Michael Newton Institute USA. I graduated and became the first certified Life Between Life therapist in Brisbane the following year after submitting my 5 case studies and I became a full member of TNI until 2012.

I have trained with many of the pioneers in spiritual regression over the years. These include, Dr Brian Weiss, The Roger Woolger Institute and I have also trained in past life regression with Dolores Cannon. I'm proud to be one of her featured practitioners on her web site. I have facilitated hundreds of clients through past life memories and beyond to the between life realms.

Like the pioneers who have come before me I began to create my own method and scripts for regression. There are many ways to regress clients to remember their past lives and Soul Regression Therapy came about through many hours of working with clients. My husband John also played a big part in the creation of this unique method of regression therapy that we now call "Soul Regression Therapy".

7. AN INTRODUCTION TO SOUL REGRESSION THERAPY

Soul Regression Therapy (SRT) is a powerful cutting edge transpersonal regression therapy that enables access to the client's subconscious mind through hypnotic regression. Memories stored in the deep subconscious or unconscious mind and physical memories stored in the body can be accessed and explored by using hypnotic regression. In regression there is a part of the mind that feels as if it is reliving the memory, while at the same time another part of the mind stays conscious and aware of the present moment and is able to describe and discuss the memory with the therapist.

Soul Regression Therapy consists of 2 separate sessions; each session is approximately 3 hours long. The first session is a Past Life Regression beginning in the current childhood, then regressing back into the womb and onto past lives. The aim of this first session is to find and resolve unconscious patterns, contracts, agreements, and complexes such as fears or phobias, body memories or tension, unexplained pain that may come from past lives that are negatively affecting the present quality of the client's life. By exploring past lives we can see beyond the confusion and illusions of the present life to bring about a healing that can resonate quantumly into the present life and beyond.

Vows or soul contracts may still be running unconsciously and affect relationships in the current life. Often we re-create similar experiences unconsciously in the current life as an attempt to complete or heal an unresolved past life experience. The aim is to help the client to understand the connection between their past life and their present life issues and clear any unwanted karma. And also help the client to understand the lessons of their past life personalities so that they can stop the pattern recurring.

The second session is more advanced and involves a hypnotic regression that takes the client directly to a past life, but at the death in the past life the soul journey continues into the spirit world, between life or Bardo realm. This the place the soul calls home. For most clients it is best they have experienced a successful past life regression first before attempting to go further into deeper subconscious memories. When clients experience a past life regression first, this helps them to prepare and develop the mind to go in to the deeper hypnotic state more easily and to eliminate any fears they may have that could prevent them from accessing these deeper hypnotic theta/delta states. This also helps to develop a rapport and trust between client and therapist which is a very important part of the process. The client is asked to bring in a list of up to 10 questions that are asked on their behalf by the therapist at appropriate stages during the session. These questions can help the client to gain an awareness of their true immortal identity, karmic lessons and their soul's purpose. Each session is unique and the client experiences something very different, there is no standard session.

The client may be greeted by a light being or spirit guide, and visit many different places once in the afterlife which include: a place of healing which may be a temple or healing chamber. They may meet with their spirit group or soul friends. Visit with Etheric Tribunal or Spiritual Masters or visit the Akashic Records. They often describe visiting a pre-conception area where they chose their next body, or parents in their next life. At the end of the session all insights and healing experienced is integrated into the client's current life.

Whether the client is a sceptic or a believer in reincarnation, almost all those who undergo a Soul Regression Therapy session are greatly moved by the experience. There are many stories that emerge from sessions and they are not all famous people, Kings or Queens, they are real people with real problems that mostly cannot be identified in the history books. Often they have lived lives where they were extremely poor, or victims of a disaster. No matter what the past life story is they always find themselves at the death scene floating up from the body knowing that life is over. After the soul has left the body they realise at this point they have the opportunity to review the life just lived, to recognise and release any unwanted patterns that they may still be repeating in the current life. They also have the opportunity to forgive any perpetrators and to forgive themselves for any wrong doings they may have done.

8. UNDERSTANDING DEATH AND BIRTH

LORNA'S VIEW

For most of my life I have been on a quest to understand life, death and birth. From my metaphysical studies and from witnessing firsthand the death scenes of hundreds of my client's sessions I believe I have gained a good understanding of death. Death is not to be feared and is only a name given to the phenomenon of when the soul leaves the physical body. Death is only the withdrawal of the soul from the physical senses and the soul's entrance to the etheric realms of consciousness.

A metaphor of death is the snake as it sheds its skin or the caterpillar when it changes into a beautiful butterfly. We shed the physical garment, the body and simply move from one state to another, it does not mean the end. Death is just a transition from one realm to another and we are never alone because we are greeted by loved ones who have gone before us.

Many of my clients describe death as when the soul begins to withdraw from the body starting at the soles of the feet and ending with the top of the head. The whole body becomes numb and when all of the soul has collected at the point between the eyebrows breathing stops and so does all the bodily functions. At that point the soul leaves the body and the body ceases to live. Usually once the soul has left the physical body it feels relief and is ready to transition to the next level of existence, describing a feeling of release as the soul departs the body and begins floating away. The soul doesn't want to hang around and is ready to go to the next realm of existence. Often describing moving down a long dark, breathing, living tunnel of energy and entering into a white light. Or drifting up into a dark sky with galaxies and stars, souls are then reunited with family members who have passed into spirit before them and they remember who they are on a soul level. Family members are waiting to greet them and welcome the soul back home. Often there are many people waiting and these people are described as being a part of their soul family.

Consider how it is for us when we are born, it is a very similar experience to this. The child comes down a long dark, living breathing tunnel, called the birth canal. At the end of the birth canal is a bright light, and the new born child doesn't know anyone as it arrives into this new world. It can feel scary and as the child leaves the birth canal they cry out and all their family is there to greet them. Their Mother, Father, sisters, brothers, all come forward to welcome the new baby/soul into the world. The soul is stepping into a readymade family, who will take care of them and keep them safe.

One of these experiences is called being born, and the other is called dying. Think of it this way, when we die, are we really dying? From observing my clients experiences we seem really happy to leave and go back home, and when we are born we are apprehensive and unsure and cry because we don't remember who we really are and where we are going and why. In my opinion, from all the research I have done on this subject over the years, death is actually an easier experience than birth. We only know birth as birth because we believe what we are told about it and similarly we know death as death for the same reason. Where do these beliefs come from, why are we told this? The answer is because this is what Christianity and society wants us to believe, and there is now a large body of evidence that says otherwise.

It is a medical fact that after a new born baby is born and takes its first breath, the ductus arteriosus in the child's heart closes over, this change is normal in newborns. This artery never changes again until the point of death, when the last breath is taken, then it opens again and closes for the last time as the person releases the last breath and dies. This automatic action of the hearts valve opens at birth and closes again at death and makes me wonder that perhaps the body is taking in something and then letting it out again, if this is the case, could this be the way the soul enters the physical body at birth and then exits as the body dies?

9. REALMS OF SOUL EXISTENCE

According to ancient teachings there are several levels of existence the soul moves through after death to evolve, these are called realms. These realms are more easily understood when we simplify them into 3.

Lower Astral or Physical Realm

This is the realm the soul resides in when in the physical body and is a sensory place of time and space. This is where our consciousness is focused and is the place the soul reincarnates into to work out karma and is also the place where fragments of the soul can be left behind and seen as ghosts.

Spirit or Astral Realm

This is the intermediate realm and is the spirit realm where souls reside. It is the place the Sharman views in trance and the dreamtime of the Aboriginal people. This is also a realm of confusion and of heaven and hell, of dreams, astral travellers and is a transitory state. The experience the soul has in this realm is based on the programmed beliefs the person dies with. When we die we take our thoughts, emotions and baggage with us. We are the creators of our own reality in this realm.

Divine Astral Realm

The highest of the realms is the divine realm and the world of pure light. This is the world of spirit guides, ascended Masters, and angelic beings. This is the true home of all spirit soul energies and is a timeless realm that is often referred to as heaven, the afterlife or Bardo.

The Between Life or Bardo Realms

The Afterlife or Bardo is the belief that all souls ascend to a spirit place or realm between lives, either between lives on earth or lives on other planets or realms. It is known as a spiritual plane where all souls go to plan and prepare for the next life or incarnation, to reconnect with their spirit friends, to rest, to heal from a difficult or traumatic life, to learn, to meet with spiritual advisors. It is the time between lives that allows the soul to consider karmic destiny and make choices that will best fulfil that destiny. Think of it this way: as one door opens and another door closes, what happens in the hallway or corridors between doors?

The Tibetans have always been aware of the afterlife and in "The Book of the Dead" the interlife is known as the Bardo. The Egyptians are also well known for their focus on the afterlife and reincarnation as part of their religion and in daily life, as do the Hindu and the Buddhist religions.

10. PROOF THE SOUL EXISTS

Many people like to have some form of evidence and often ask me can we prove the existence of the soul and there are a few ways we can do this. One is the near death experience many people have, this is when the person has stopped breathing and the functions of the heart and brain have ceased. They are pronounced clinically dead, but for some reason they are revived and many explain what was going on around them even though the heart had stopped and there was no brain activity. This suggests that consciousness can be considered to be separate from the brain and body, which provides a basis for claims of reincarnation and the existence of the soul. This phenomenon has been documented by Dr Raymond Moody in his books about life after death and near-death experiences (NDE), a term that he coined in 1975 in his best-selling book Life After Life.

There is a hard core of cases involving children and adults who have reported detailed and factual information so obscure that they could not have known this information any other way. There are many documented cases where children have spontaneously remembered their past lives without any prompting. One well documented case is of a girl from India called Shanti Devi, she was born in 1926 and died 1987. Shanty claimed to remember details of a past life where she lived as a woman called Lugdi Devi who died 10 days after giving birth; she lived in a village close to her home in Deli. This case received so much attention that Mahatma Gandhi set up a commission to investigate the claims. The commission's report concluded that Shanti Devi was indeed the reincarnation of Lugdi Devi. When she was about 4 years old, she told her parents that her real home was in Mathura where her husband lived, about 145 km from her home in Dehli. Discouraged by her parents, she ran away from home at age 6, trying to reach Mathura. Back home, she stated in school that she was married and had died 10 days after having given birth to a child.

A psychiatrist named Ian Stevenson researched this case in detail. Stevenson became known internationally for his research into reincarnation, and he believed that emotions, memories, and even physical injuries in the form of birthmarks, can be transferred from one life to another. His research spanned over 40 years investigating 3,000 cases of children around the world who claimed to remember past lives. Through his research he came to believe that certain phobias, unusual abilities and illnesses could not be explained by heredity or the environment. He believed that personality transfer provided a type of explanation and he wrote many books outlining his research into this subject.

People often ask me are there enough souls to go around? I believe that there is an endless supply of souls and many are coming back to Earth more rapidly, this is because Earth needs more people to help shift the negative energy to a more positive vibration. Many souls are volunteering to come to help heal this planet. We have been harming the finely balanced environment of Earth for centuries and it's time now to make some changes to our attitude and the way we treat our planetary home or we will destroy our magnificent physical home along with every living thing on it. Human life on Earth is also only one small part of the universal cosmos and many souls are coming to here for the first time to help with this shift.

11. KARMIC DESTINY

We cannot escape the laws of karma and once we understand this law then we begin to understand why some people are unhappy and others are not. Why some are poor and others are rich and we can begin to comprehend many of the so called injustices of the world. That what happens to us is really a direct result of our actions and thoughts and we cannot avoid this law because it is very powerful and applies to everyone.

There are 2 ways we can view the universe we live in, we can either believe that everything that happens is random and that we evolved to our present state by accident and when we die we become nothing, which would suggest that life is actually meaningless. Or we can take the view that there is some sort of grand hidden plan that was created by a high intelligence. You could call this intelligence God, Allah, Universal Mind, Jesus, Budda, the Architect, the collective unconscious, Source or any name that is right for you. Now if there is a grand plan then wouldn't it make sense that justice would be part of that plan? But most people feel there is no justice in life on earth. Where is the justice in poverty, misery, child abuse, murders, war, rape? I believe that karma explains all of this in a very logical way and puts all this in perspective by explaining the reason for the inequalities in life very well.

Karma is a multi-life debt system, that rewards and punishes beyond the current life and is a total justice system. Everything that you think, say and do creates or erases karma including your motives, intent and desire. When you believe in karma this means that you have to take full responsibility for yourself, you are responsible for everything that has happened to you. You are your own judge and jury and your soul is aware that in order for you to progress spiritually you must experience many things in order to learn the lessons you have set for yourself before your birth.

The fastest way to learn is to fully experience the consequences of all your actions. You can no longer blame anyone for your life because the concept of blame is incompatible with the belief in karma. The ex-partner who caused you so much pain, the person who deceived you on the internet and took all your money even, your parents, or children who disowned you. As controversial as it may seem you created these entire events and attracted all these people into your life because you needed the balance and test.

If you take a moment and think back over your lifetime and remember everyone from your past who made your life difficult. These people have helped you to accomplish your goal of spiritual evolution and to balance out your karma. They came into your life to help you to determine how you are progressing spiritually. The way to tell if you are passing your own tests or failing them is to ask yourself how do you currently respond to these memories, people and situations? Do you respond with love, positive thoughts, compassion, can you let go of the past and the emotions from it? If you can, then you are passing the test. But if not, and you are hanging on to resentment, revenge, blame, anger, hate, then you are failing, but this is all right, because you will be given an opportunity to come back and live another life with a similar theme so that you can do this in another way. Some souls don't even have to wait to balance this out in another life time, they are given the opportunity to balance the karma in the current life time as well.

Sir Isaac Newton who has been considered by many to be the greatest and most influential scientist who ever lived expresses the principal that for every action there is an equal and opposite reaction. This is called the law of action and reaction, cause and effect or karma, which is a Sanskrit word that means action. Many of our past actions have shaped our current situations in life and this includes our actions in past lives as well. Once we understand this we can begin to take personal responsibility for all our actions rather than blaming other people or blaming situations for our problems and being a victim. The problem is most people don't remember their past lives, when we are born we come into life with amnesia, nature has given us the blessing of not remembering.

We are spiritual beings who have chosen to experience life in a physical universe, and once we are immersed in life we forget who we really are. Just imagine having perfect recall, remembering every single thing you have ever read, ate, thought, smelt, saw and heard. You couldn't function with that mass of material in your mind. The past is valuable and is what makes you the person that you are today. Most people act and react due to the experiences of their past lives but these experiences are usually unconscious. We forget who we were at birth and what we did in our past lives, but we are presented with the lessons from the past and they are repeated in current and future lives until learned. A hard life can be chosen in order to remind ourselves of the important things in life. If someone chooses a life of pain and feeling unloved and uncared for, it is possible that this is because they want to always remember how it feels to feel so sad, so that they avoid making others feel that way. If we experience the negative, we can truly understand the benefits of the positive.

Reincarnation evidence indicates that we all need to learn how to move away from fear based emotions and attitudes towards ones based more on love and understanding. But in order for us to truly understand the negative properly we need to experience it for ourselves. For how can we truly know how others feel until we have walked in their shoes?

12. SOUL CONTRACTS

The soul leaves the physical garment at the point of death and journeys back to the spiritual realms from where it came. The soul carries with it an imprint of all the memories of all the lives and experiences ever lived. Once home in spirit the soul has the opportunity to debrief with spiritual guides and advisors who help the returning soul to fully understand the life just lived and left behind. Sometimes we may visit with a council/panel of wise elders or Master guides. We may receive advice of needing to repeat something we didn't learn in the immediate past life and if this is the case then we may have to live through a similar life or experience until we really learn this lesson. Earth is really a school where souls come to learn lessons, it's similar to enrolling in a course and if we don't pass then we need to revisit the course or class again until we pass.

Our spirit guides help us to work out if we passed the test or not and also to choose our next life. This is not a punishment because we have free will even when we are in spirit, we can choose to stay in spirit for as long as we like, but eventually we are encouraged by our guides to reincarnate again because until we do we will not be able to progress spiritually and return to the source of our creation. The soul learns best from hardships and pain, this is why we experience difficult lives.

Our parents, careers, relationships, major events, including sorrows and joys are all selected in advance in the interlife. We decide our next soul contracts or karmic scripts. We choose the lessons we want to learn, we analyse what went wrong in our last incarnation when we go back home to spirit and plan for the next life time. This is so that we can ensure we have opportunities to resolve unfinished issues within ourselves or with others. The price of advancement is not through living an easy life but through challenges and difficulty. Often the soul will make a contract with another soul to learn specific lessons. An example of this is; a man intentionally beats and harms his wife so that she can't leave him, and he causes her to be a cripple. The person who caused this to happen might have to take another life to face the consequences of what he did and understand how it feels to be controlled, beaten and crippled. This person may return to a life where the roles are reversed between these souls. Because this action was deliberate the unavoidable result could be some sort of unfortunate experience that could even cause the person to be born crippled in some way and then cared for or controlled by the other person.

In past life therapy clients may remember once again the terrible hurts, the loss, death and pain of times past. This work is not easy and tears often flow. But these are cathartic tears that wash and cleanse the soul. Therapy without tears is like bathing without water. Often the most painful lessons of the past are the ones that teach us the most in the present. Growing through these lessons is what brings true wisdom. For wisdom is but having learned to grow from a myriad of incarnations.

Past life therapy helps people to be more balanced, to be more responsible, to gain emotional and spiritual maturity and a sense of their own true worth. By understanding our past lives and the lessons we set for ourselves we gain an overview of the soul's journey and purpose. The soul's goal is to learn, to improve, expand and unfold into a more whole, healthy and happy person. Spiritual development is what Earth school is all about. As children in school we seldom think of the reasons for being there and even less about our purposes and ideals. We are there because we have to be there to learn our lessons. There is another reason for remembering past lives, a lot of benefit can come from remembering and reliving happy experiences, times of great love and accomplishment.

For me integrating my present life and my past has not been easy, it's taken a long time to understand the complexities of my various lifetimes. I have tried to condense the essence of each life into its most important parts and I have searched for the reasons for each life and the most important lessons. I then try to form this into a whole new picture, to bring all the varied parts and experiences together to get an overview. I then take time to meditate on how the past fits into my present and where my present fits into my past. I look for alternative ways to build upon lessons learnt and create a better future. Many insights have come from this process; my biggest insight I have discovered is what I dislike in others is often a part of myself, either in a past life or my present life. Through gaining this insight I can now see facets of myself reflected in other people and I have come to understand that many of my problems are self-created.

When a person dies different experiences may await the soul, being reborn on earth is only one of them and reincarnation suggests that the soul may have to return to this plane of consciousness to account for deeds done in the past. I now view life as an unlimited school, with the different grades as different life times. Because when we study and learn, we pass our tests and we progress, by neglecting our studies and failing our tests we have to take them over and over again until we pass. But in this school of life we have with us an innate "in-tuition", "in" meaning inner and "tuition" meaning teacher, in other words we are our own teacher, and we can grade our own tests and progress gained with the help of our guides when we go back to spirit.

Although my work is extremely challenging and I often witness highly emotional states in my clients, I would never change what I do. I know that I am exceptionally privileged to be able to explore the past lives of my clients and then to join them on the soul's journey to the afterlife. I view this work to be a great honour, to be alongside my client's and to behold their immortal soul's essence and one that I will be eternally grateful for.

13. SOUL FAMILIES AND SOUL MATES

Soul mates are the people whom we share a special bond with over many life times and make up our small close soul family. This group is usually made up of soul mates that help each other to learn important spiritual lessons. We all have primary soul mates that are usually a closely bonded partner, lover, friend or close family members. Primary soul mates are very important and often we reincarnate with them through many lifetimes so that we can work out our karmic lessons. Often it's difficult to recognise some of these soul family members when meeting them in a Soul Regression – between life session, this is because they may not be in our current life now, they may have been born in different decades or they could be souls mates from different realms of existence.

Relationship issues are a common reason why people come for a past life regression. People may want to know why they haven't been able to have a long term relationship or why their husband left them for someone else, or why their partner died. Today it is possible to have several soul mate relationship opportunities in one lifetime and each relationship offers an opportunity to master different lessons. Sometimes when soul mates meet in the current lifetime circumstances may prevent them from pursuing a love relationship, so they honour an agreement to only meet and then to part.

Some limiting circumstances that keep romantic soul mates apart may be, age differences, being born into the same family. Or born the same gender or unwilling to pursue a same gender love relationship, one partner already has a relationship or family they can't abandon, or there may be cultural or religious differences. When my clients first meet with their soul family members in the afterlife they often describe seeing them as bright sparks of lights moving towards them and surrounding them. Often 1 or 2 of these soul mates will come forward with messages or they might have a conversation with them and understand their relationships over many lives. Meeting with soul family members is a very healing experience.

14. SOUL REGRESSION THERAPY CASE STUDIES

Note

The following chapters contain case studies from my client's sessions that I have selected for this book. Some are of past life regression sessions and others are regressions to the afterlife. By reading these case studies it is my hope that you may identify with them and this book will inspire you to break the shackles that may be binding you to an unfulfilled life. To break free and to take a risk to create the life you want for yourself. And if you need help this may lead you to seek out a professionally trained Soul Regression Therapist.

15. GUILT AND PAIN

PENNY'S STORY

PART 1 – PAST LIFE

Your task is not to seek for love, but merely to seek and find all the barriers within yourself that have been built against it. Jelaluddin Rumi, 13th century Sufi

Penny came to see me for a past life regression after attending a psychic fair. At the fair she had received a tarot reading by a psychic who told her that she had past life karma that needed to be cleared. Penny didn't know what this meant because she had never given any thought to past lives before. She did have a belief in reincarnation even though she didn't fully understand. She had never had a psychic reading done before. For 20 years she had been a part of the Pentecostal church and they didn't approve of psychics or past lives. Penny had become very disillusioned with their views and had finally left the church.

I have seen many clients who have been recommended to me by psychics who saw their clients past lives in a reading. A good psychic is able to pick up on past lives as well as the future, many psychics are unable to clear the contracts so they send their clients to see a past life regression therapist like myself.

During the pre-talk before the session began, Penny began

to tell me about her life. She had divorced her husband Graham over 15 years ago and was now happily married to Paul. She had 3 children to her ex-husband and all of them were born with Asperger syndrome and Graham also had Asperger syndrome. Wikipedia states that; "Asperger syndrome is an autism spectrum disorder that is characterized by significant difficulties in social interaction, alongside restricted and repetitive patterns of behaviour and interests. It differs from other autism spectrum disorders by its relative preservation of linguistic and cognitive development. Although not required for diagnosis, physical clumsiness and atypical (peculiar, odd) use of language are frequently reported. The syndrome is named after the Austrian paediatrician Hans Asperger who, in 1944, studied and described children in his practice who lacked nonverbal communication skills, demonstrated limited empathy with their peers, and were physically clumsy".

Life had been extremely difficult for Penny, her children were difficult to manage and she didn't receive much support from her ex-husband. She eventually left him because she felt like she had a 4th child. He failed to tell her he had Asperger syndrome until their youngest son was diagnosed; she was very confused and began to question him about why all their children were affected. If he had told her before they were married she would not have had 3 children with him. She described her 3 children as being very clever but socially inept. They are adults now and have left home, and she has no contact with them because she felt she needed a well-earned break, especially now that she was remarried. She had cared for all of them for 25 years and was feeling extremely burnt out mentally, emotionally and physically. Penny was now married to Paul and they had been together for 15 years, they had a son Chris who was 13 and she described him as being a normal healthy boy. She was happy to be a stay at home mum enjoying a much quieter life these days with her new family.

Penny's childhood was also very difficult. She believed her parents didn't want her and her mother had told her she had considered an abortion. Her mother was only 18 when she accidently fell pregnant with Penny, not long after her parents had a shot gun wedding. They operated a service station and cafe where the family lived in the back of the premises for 7 years. Penny and her younger brother were left to fend for themselves for most of the time while their parents worked long hours. She said, "they never had time for me or my brother and I became like a mother to him." As she grew older, her relationship with her parents became strained and she had not had any contact with them for 14 years. Her mother had fostered a lot of children over the years, but it was like she had forgotten she had 2 of her own.

Penny also had a skin condition called rosacea which started just before she married Paul. At first she thought the rash was hormonal, but after a few years she went to a doctor who diagnosed the rash as rosacea, this a chronic condition characterized by facial redness and sometimes pimples and can affect all ages. It primarily affects Caucasians of north western European descent and affects both sexes, but is almost 3 times more common in women. It has a peak age of onset between 30 and 60. Penny had tried many different types of treatments for her skin condition over the years but it still persisted.

She also told me that she had grown very close to Paul's late mother when she was alive, and considered her like her own mother; she took great interest in her children. Penny was with her when she died of a stroke in her late fifties. Her mother-in-law had come through with a message in the psychic reading which had surprised Penny. She described her life so far as a journey she would rather not have taken. Even though she was divorced, her ex-husband still caused her problems, often accusing her of being an unfit mother. Her youngest son had left home recently and she hadn't had time to think about what life would be like without all the chains around her.

She went on to explain, "my family try to drag me down with the constant insults and it's like I haven't yet had a chance to live my life without them." She spoke about her eldest daughter Susan and how she felt a strong bond between them. Even though she is estranged from Susan, she grieves for her every day. She felt they had been together in past lives. Penny's relationship to her youngest child Chris was very different to her relationships with her other children. "Chris is my son to Paul; he is very easy to love because he gives love back. To have a little boy who is so full of love and kindness is just so completely odd to me. I gave out love and got nothing back for all my life."

As Penny's story unfolded I began to see a theme emerging. A theme of a lack of feeling loved that started even before she was born, when her mother became pregnant with her and was forced to marry her father. This theme had continued into a loveless marriage with her ex-husband and a one sided relationship with her 3 Asperger syndrome children. She felt that love was alien to her and even though she was now married to Paul she felt he was more of a father figure, a provider of stability in her life rather than her soul mate. "Even though Paul constantly tells me he loves me, I just don't know how to accept love" she said. I explained to her that soul mates are not always romantic partners and we can have many in our lives, they are usually in our life to help us to learn an important lesson. She said she understood this now. She had learnt patience from being married to her ex-husband and bringing up their Asperger syndrome children; patience was something she knew well. Although her life had felt like hell on earth she could see the good in it and she was aware of some of the lessons she had already learnt. But she wanted to know more about her soul's karmic journey and the reasons for all the pain and suffering. She also wanted to know if she had lived any past lives with her daughter Susan and her husband Paul.

Because Penny had never experienced hypnosis before I began to explain to her what she could expect in the session. I explained that hypnosis was not sleep, but state between sleep and waking. A natural brain wave cycle or state the brain goes into throughout the day. The brain goes through 4 cycles every day, Delta is the deepest level it's the realm of sleep, Beta is the wake cycle, alpha and theta are the cycles in between and are the hypnotic cycles.

Hypnosis is not sleep or a coma, her brain would still be awake but slightly relaxed, like in a day dream but her body may feel like it's heavy and asleep. Her fingers and toes may tingle and her eyes may water a little. These are all natural signs of hypnosis and hypnosis is a natural state, a hypnotherapist can't make someone's brain do something that is doesn't already do, that's not possible. A hypnotherapist knows how to take a person into this state if the person allows it.

Penny felt comfortable with me and entered into a deep hypnotic state very easily, as evident by the rapid movement of her eyes under her eyelids. I began guiding her back through time to remember a far memory of a past life that would help her to understand her current life better. As she began to describe her soundings and what was happening her voice sounded a little stressed.

P: It's very cold here and I'm wearing brown boots and a big long coat with fur around the hood. I'm a young 13-year-old girl and my name is Claudia, Its Germany and it's winter, I'm walking along a track through the forest, the wind is blowing in the trees, it's so cold but it's not snowing yet, it's too cold to snow.

As we progressed Claudia told me she had come to the edge of the forest and could see a tiny village ahead in a valley. She began walking down to the village and as she reached the village she described walking on slippery cobble stones;

P: They are slippery because it's so cold.

She was going to her grandmother's house and described the houses along the way looked like gingerbread houses painted white, with wooden beams.

P: I'm caring a basket with bread, with a cover over it. I'm at the steps now and she is waiting at the front door for me.

Her voice became softer and quiet; I love her so much, Grandmother is round and she hugs me and I stay hugged, it's like she takes all the breath out of me. We sit down and she has a stew cooking in a big pot on a wooden stove and she serves me some with the bread that I brought.

At this point she tells me she lives with her grandmother because her parents didn't want her when she was born. The scene changes again quickly and she remembered another time where Claudia was 23. Her grandmother had just died. She recognised her grandmother was the same soul as her grandmother in her current life a Penny. Her grandmother was buried in the local cemetery in the village where she lived. Claudia could see her grandmothers grave from the window in her house, she wanted it there so that she could see it. I asked her to describe the engraving on the grave stone, as she replied her voice changed and she began to speak with a slight German accent.

P: Its Gretchen, Claudia's grandmother 1768, I live alone now... I don't marry... I work in a laundry... I live in Olsten and my life is very lonely now my Grandmother is gone.

I moved her forward to age 50 and she describes her life in more details but she is still living alone.

P: There was a scandal with my parents and everyone in the village knew, I'm ashamed and I prefer to be on my own, because my parents abandoned me. My parents were gypsies and they lived in a gypsy wagon, they left me when I was born with my grandmother. It's shameful to have gypsies in the family. They ran off together even though they weren't married, it's best to be thought of as dead.

We moved to the last day of Claudia's life and she died in the same bed her grandmother died, at age 72.

P: I have a fever... I feel sick... my hair is white now. It's over and it's peaceful, I'm floating over the village, I see the whole village They are burying me with my grandmother, there's a funeral but there's no one there. It was sad because I was always alone, alone at death and I was alone as a child.

L: *How do you feel about your death and do you have any regrets about that life?*

P: I'm glad it's over... but I regret not getting married and having my own family, I cared for my grandmother and worked hard and I never brought shame to my family.

As Claudia died and her soul left the body she connected to the higher part of herself, this part is sometimes known as the Higher Self or Soul Self, and knows everything about us and can answer any question asked. Below is the dialogue which followed from Penny's higher Self.

P: She has the same abandonment issues as Penny, her grandmother raised her in both lifetimes, her parents brought disgrace to the family in both lifetimes and she still carries hurt for things that were not hers and guilt for things that were not her fault. This is a theme through many past lives. She cannot take responsibility for the actions of other people; a child cannot be responsible for the actions of the parent.

I was amazed with the profoundness and wisdom that comes through Penny, her voice had now changed, she speaks clearly and with certainty.

P: Penny keeps herself shut away just like Claudia did. Claudia missed out on so much life because she would not go out; she held guilt that no one else saw but her. She does the same thing now as Penny. Penny needs to try to get out just a little; she needs to be able to be loved, to let people love her. Claudia never married because she wouldn't let anyone love her. She has been with Paul before; he had always cared, protected and loved her. He is in her life now because now it's time for her to be loved, he is very special. She needs to start to live, she has been burdened for so long, and now the burden has been lifted. She needs to live and if she will just take Pauls hand it will be okay. He won't take her anywhere that will hurt her. He just wants to show her how to live. Her lesson is to not take on the guilt which is not hers; this is a high level lesson.

L: *Can you explain this in more detail?*

P: The lesson she is learning from her children is also guilt. They made her feel guilty, the same guilt, she was put down and could do nothing right, she was put down by her children. And people would mock her because of her children. She chose the life as Penny, but it was too much to take on in one lifetime. She wasn't equipped to deal with what she took on, she was impatient. She sacrificed another life to get it all done, many sacrificed lives. If she gets it right in the life of Penny she won't have to repeat it again. The cause of the rosacea is from sadness, because she can't accept that Paul loves her, she's more comfortable if he goes away. She's more comfortable with rejection. She knows how to deal with loneliness, as Claudia did. And she knows how to live those types of lives. She doesn't know how to live a life with love.

I asked her higher mind to help Penny to allow love to come into her, to open up her heart to Paul. To accept his love and to begin to step out and slowly begin to allow love and let people in. She is stuck in this pattern, and now she has the opportunity to break this theme.

P: She needs to know that she can give love and that she actually deserves to get love back. She's never got love back; it's always been one way.

L: *Has she ever lived a life where she had received love?*

P: Yes, there was a life where she had the love of a father who adored her. Her daughter Susan is like Penny, she doesn't feel worthy of love. She is loved so much but she doesn't feel it, she's like Claudia. She is very head strong; Penny has cared for Susan in many lives, like Claudia cared for her grandmother. Penny must be patient with her daughter, she knows patience and the bond is so strong. The lesson she was to learn with Graham was patience and he was to learn responsibility, it was agreed. He is part of her soul family as well as Paul, also her son Chris and Susan.

Her voice changed again and Penny began to speak;

P: I see Susan... she is a bright light, she is very special to me. My mother is here too, she is at the back but I see those I recognise at the front and at the back is my mother. It's like she is hiding from me, I don't want to hear her.

Penny's mother began to speak.

P: I taught you independence, Claudia and Caroline didn't need to learn independence... I taught you independence.

At this stage Penny remembered another of her past lives, she had been a little girl whose father loved her dearly.

P: He spoiled me, and I wanted for nothing but I wasn't independent.

This life as Caroline was the life before she was Penny and the year was 1856.

P: I was loved too much, I lived in England. I didn't have a mother, only a father. My father is the soul of my brother Ray in my current life.

I am amazed at the detail in which she is viewing and understanding this and wait for her to continue, there is no need for questions, I am merely a witness to the vivid past lives she is describing.

P: Caroline had everything, as I grew older I married the soul of Paul, she explains to me. It was a wonderful life; I was so loved and wanted for nothing. I came from a family of great importance, a big manor house. I was spoilt by my father and my husband. My father had lots of land. I died from a fall from a horse and hurt my head,

I was not old. She went on to explain; ah, very sad, Paul is heartbroken, he is leaning over me and he was riding too and is heartbroken. I died in his arms, it was so quick, I hit my head, he is wailing, he can't speak... he's holding me up... all that sadness, it's so sad.

P: That life was too short we didn't have enough time, so we have come back together to bring that love. Her ability to switch between the unconscious mind that recounts the memory and the conscious mind which is able to explain and analyse at the same time is very fascinating to observe and happens quite often with somnambulistic people. Caroline was 30 when she died, Paul came back to Penny at the same age when she was 30; Penny was the same age as Caroline when he came into her life. He came back to bring that love, he came back. Caroline made a choice that was wrong, and that's not how fate should have been. She shouldn't have been on that horse. He was sad because she was with child, she shouldn't have been on the horse. You have got to accept love, because if she had listened she would not have died. She was told not to ride the horse, she was told in love but she still couldn't accept it even though Caroline was surrounded by so much love from her husband and her father.

Penny was beginning to realise that her lesson was to accept the love she deserves. Even criticisms if they are given with love and in her best interest. She also began to make soul connections to the people who were in her past lives and in her current life as Penny.

Her Higher Self began speaking again; "the baby Caroline lost when she died from the fall off her horse is Penny's son Chris. Caroline's nanny was Paul's mother. She helped raised her and was like a mother to her, she was very special. She is also part of

Penny's soul family and she said you have to learn to let go. Penny needs to listen and take advice and if she lets people in and they hurt her, it's nothing more than the hurt she has inflicted on herself. She's got to try. Her rosacea will clear up very soon, when she realises it's okay to be loved. And it's okay to be attractive and it's okay to let people get close. She uses it to frighten people away. It's like an outward sign that you can't love me because of the way I look. When she lets people get close and she loves her self and lets people love her then it won't matter anymore."

PENNY'S STORY CONTINUES
PART 2- BETWEEN LIVES

John facilitated Penny's second session a few months later. Penny was really pleased with her first session and quite surprised with all the information she was able to remember. But she wanted to find out more details about her past lives, and she also wanted to know more about the afterlife. There are 2 parts to a Soul Regression Therapy session, the second session is advanced because the client is guided through a past life and then onto the afterlife where they often meet with their soul family, spirit guides and they can find out a lot of information about their immortal soul's journey.

Penny drifted into a deep hypnotic state very easily, and she quickly regressed to a past life. I didn't need to ask many questions, I just let her talk, only asking questions when appropriate.

J: *Where are you now?*

P: Its morning and the sun is just coming up. I'm on a huge boat coming into the harbour to our new home, and I feel very excited because we have emigrated. It's a huge ship and I'm a little girl age 7, and this is such a big adventure. My father is standing next to me and I'm wearing black lace up boots and I have my best dress on, it's linen. I have to have my best dress on because this is very important. I don't have a mother, I'm with my father and he is very dapper. My name is Margaret Elizabeth O'Connell, my father calls me Maggie. We are coming into Sydney harbour and the year is 1903.

As she processes the images, she continued.

P: We have left Ireland and this is our new home, this will be a new start. I get sick and it was always so cold and my health will improve now. My father will start a new business and we are going to start a new life here. My father is very loving and he wants the best for me, his name is Albert. I can breathe so much easier here already, the warmth and the salt air fill my lungs and it feels so fresh.

The scene changed quickly and she moved to the last day of Maggie's life;

P: I'm age 20 now and I'm walking home, there is such a high step between the road and the footpath... I'm walking along and carrying a carpet bag. My father owns a business down on the wharfs, he's a trader, his business helps to unload and reload the ships that come in and I work for him. I'm carrying a carpet bag that has money in it from my father's business and it's over my shoulder and I'm taking it home, it's starting to get dark. I have it held really tightly, her voice changed and she sounded scared, there are 2 men who are walking behind me now, I can hear their footsteps... they have hit me on the back of my head and I have fallen, they grab the bag... it wasn't me they wanted it was the bag with the money. I'm outside my body now, I was hit very hard and I move out of the body very quickly, even before I hit the ground.

J: *What is important for you to know about this life you just lived as Maggie?*

I was wondering what lessons are to be learnt from this.

P: I learnt that my father's love meant everything to me. He gave up everything he knew to move to the other side of the world for his daughter. He started a business from scratch and he did it all for me. I learnt determination; you have to make the best of every situation. I regret that I never married; it was because I was always caught up with business matters to be social.

J: *What happens to you now?*

P: I feel an incredible pull to take me away, but I need to stay with my body just until someone comes, I don't want to leave her alone... oh there is a man coming up the street now, he's a policeman and I can go now. I feel very sad about her death, she was very young, but I can leave her now.

J: *How do you feel as you leave?*

P: I'm moving really fast it's wonderful... I'm going towards a place of light and I feel I have been here before. It looks like a fog in the distance, but in amongst the fog I can see crystals. I have slowed down now and I see purple, pink and yellow, like a single pillar that I'm moving towards. It's starting to change shape, it was like a hard pillar and now it's starting to round off and become softer. It's going all around me now, is enveloping me in light. I feel drained and it's cleansing me from the top of my head down. I have come so far and it's a long journey and it's tiering, I need to get rid of all the negative energy from that life before I can go any further. I feel I have been here before. Sometimes in the past I have been met on the way, but I know where I am going this time.

I just sit back and wait for her to continue, there is no need for questions.

P: This energy is male and is pure white light... it's like I'm going through a cleansing process and this is my first stop. I'm beginning to feel lighter now and my colour is changing, I'm white and green, and yellow now. My guide is standing off to one side. He speaks to me telepathically and said it's good to see you again. I know him well and he is changing to energy spirit form because I'm in energy spirit form. His name is Edward and he doesn't have to be in human form now, when I first saw him he was dressed in clothes that would have come from the 1800's. He's very pleased now that we are both energy form, he stays in human form because this is how I recognised him in past lives. Previously he had come down and brought me back but this time there was no need, he knows I knew the way back and he was waiting for me.

Often a spirit guide or spiritual friends come to greet the incoming soul and they may speak to the client here or take them to a special place where they meet with their personal spirit group friends or companions. This is usually made up of a special group of soul mates whose life paths are shared for a period of time, to help to learn spiritual lessons. Soul mates can be friends, lovers, family members or business partners. Today it is possible to have several soul mate relationships opportunities in one lifetime and each relationship offers an opportunity to master different lessons. Also sometimes when soul mates meet in the current lifetime circumstances may prevent them from pursuing a love relationship, so they honour an agreement to only meet and then to part.

Penny's spirit guide is called Edward and they have had past lives together.

J: *What does Edward want you to know?*

P: He's telling me the life of Maggie was an easy life, because I learnt my life lessons very early in that life. Once those lessons were learnt I was able to enjoy more of that life. And in that respect it was easy; I learnt my lessons easily and quickly. I'm in my energy state now and I'm completely cleansed and ready to move on now. Edward is taking me to a huge area, and there are lots of energies there, I know these energies it's just a quick stop.

J: *How many are there with you now?*

P: There's about 8 that are all around me and Edward is over to the right because there is no room.

J: *What's happening now?*

P: They are all around me, communicating with me at the same time. We don't speak but we communicate telepathically, they are all trying to communicate at the one time. It feels wonderful but I don't recognise them.

I'm in the middle and they are gathered around me. One of them comes forward now and I recognise him as Paul my husband and his soul name is Chiagwa. His energy is white on the outside with purple and pink and blue inside, he's beautiful.

J: *Do you have a spirit name?*

P: My spiritual name is Elesa and my energy colour is deep pink and in the centre it's purple. I also see my daughter Susan and she looks bright blue and her soul name is Kianie... Chiagwa is my soul mate and he comes as my husband Paul, and he has also been my father, always as a predominant male in my life. We agreed that was the way we would be and I am the predominant female. We don't reincarnate without each other, we always try to be together. Kianie has been my daughter, my grandmother and my mother, we just like to spend time together. She's not always female and she doesn't always reincarnate with me. The others I don't recognise, but they are all so loving towards me. We are intermediate souls, all advancing and about the same level. They have been waiting for me to return and I am so loved. They are all communicating with me at once and have lots to say... they are happy and loving.

J: *Is Edward still there with you?*

P: Yes he is now taking me to the great hall where my life books are kept. He has something to show me there.
I was wondering if this is the Akashic records many people speak about.

J: Can you describe this great hall, how does it look?

P: It's got 3 huge tables that run down the centre of this long... long room and there are bench seats even though we don't need them. To the side are cubicles where we can study privately. The benches are for public study, but the small cubicles on the side are where you study your books with your guides, this is a private place. It's a very bright place, everything is bright, from the ceilings and walls it's completely illuminated. It is a place of respect and a very important sacred place. Everyone goes there to learn from our books. This is a place of reverence and we always go there with respect always.

The most extensive source of information regarding the Akashic Records comes from the clairvoyant work of Edgar Cayce. Through hypnotic trance he was able to tap into the subconscious mind of the person he was giving a reading to and access the Akashic Records. The place in spirit where the Akashic records are located is sometimes described as being similar to a library on earth, as Penny describes it. And it contains the client's spiritual books of life. Once inside a spirit librarian or archivist may assist the soul to find their own personal life book which contains the karmic scripts for review.

J: *What's happening now?*

P: Edward is showing me my life books; he wants me to know I did very well. This is a record of the life I just lived as Maggie... I suffered adversity in that life.

J: *What do you see in this book?*

P: I can see my mother in my book... from that lifetime as Maggie, I recognise her as Cathy (Cathy is one of Penny's daughters in her current life). My mother died when I was aged 2... she was always ill and coughing, that's why my father moved us from Ireland to Australia, he was worried I would succumb to the same illness that killed my mother.

J: *Did your father care for you after your mother died?*

P: I had a nanny, she cared for me and she was very loving, but my mother only tolerated me. I recognise my nanny in my book... she is my mother-in-law in my current life as Penny, Paul's mother. She has been with me through many lifetimes and she always very loves towards me.

J: *What else do you see in your book?*

P: Edward is showing me my father's grief at my passing, but he will be alright, he was heartbroken. He's also pointing out to me right from the beginning of that book that I am loved, I am constantly loved.

Sometimes the Akashic records are seen as a computer that contains files, and I ask her to describe how the book looks to her.

P: It's like a huge photo album, I can see the photos and feel the feelings and hear the speech as if I am there. I understand now that I have dealt with not having a mother in many of my past lives. And the rejection from my mother in my current life is no different to what I have experienced in the past. She fulfilled the role of mother and once I was born that's where it ended. Maggie's mother was Cathy my daughter in my current life and Claudia's mother was my mother in my current life, but I don't recognise Caroline's mother.

She was now making connections between the people who were in her past lives.

P: I have come to this library because I want to learn from my past lives before I make my life selection for the next life. I go over and over and over my past lives so I can make the correct selections so that I can advance. Edward is with me while I do this research and he is always with me.

J: *What are you learning from your books?*

P: I'm learning compassion, it's important to learn compassion for others so that I can come back in my next life with compassion for others. This is very important to me. I study my own lives to see how I could have done better, to improve. This is a work in progress, because Claudia was too compassionate and she had no life because of the compassion she showed to another person. Caroline was not compassionate enough because she didn't understand how her actions affected other people. Maggie went the opposite way, she showed great compassion for her father, she always supported and encouraged him. It's all about balance and it's important to get that balance right and it can take many lives to learn this.

She explains that Edward wants to take her to meet with a panel of higher guides.

P: They are not judges... they don't judge me. We agree to go there and we are there now. It's instant, because we have both agreed to go. We are there now before a big wooden door with a lion's head engraved into it.

The doors are closed, and they open automatically... why they need to have doors I don't know, I think it's just symbolic.

Her analytical mind came in here, but it didn't cause any problems, and she instantly switched back to describing her experience to me.

P: I am now standing in front of the panel and Edward is slightly behind me to my left.

J: *Can you describe who is on this panel?*

P: There are 5 beings and they are in the form of energy, not human form. There is a strong feeling of love in this room that would knock you over if you were in human form. They are not here to judge because they understand how hard it is to be in human for, they know all about the trials and tribulations as a human on earth was, they have reincarnated before. They know that we don't remember we were in spirit form and there is nothing you could have done or said while in human form that they haven't done or said. They have complete compassion and understanding for all those who go before them

J: *What are they doing?*

P: They are sitting behind a long curved crescent shaped table and there is a lion's head in profile carved into the table and I'm standing in front of them. They look like they are wearing robes, but in spirit form they don't have any shape. There are male and females, but it's not a gender issue they just appear this way. The male in the middle is wearing a robe with gold trim and around his forehead is gold, he is far more advanced as a soul, and he has to be held in great respect. The female to the far right, her robe is purple and the female to the far left her robe is crimson. The 2 males on either side are wearing deep royal blue robes. The panel members are different to the last time I was here, they change after every incarnation and as I advance. This is because we have to discuss different things and what is relevant to a new soul is not relevant to a more advanced or intermediate soul.

J: *Who speaks to you first?*

P: The female on the far right, we discuss compassion because this is very important for me and is my life lesson. She is telling me about the life I just left as Maggie and says I have done well. The panel suggest to Edward that I am ready to be more challenged in my future life selection. The life as Maggie was a little bit on the easy side. I could have achieved more had I had a better life selection. They are directing this advice towards Edward not me, because he guides me through the life selection. They suggest that I chose a more challenging life next time so that I can progress quicker. Maggie's life was a challenge in the early years but then there were no more opportunities to learn the life lesson.

J: *How do you feel about what they have said to you?*

P: When I visited the panel after the life as Caroline I was chastised, I left knowing I had a lot of work to do. I was so very self-centred in that life. I had a life of great abundance but I didn't have any understanding of others around me. I was told by the panel that I could have done a lot better. I'm being told that I am to continue with the lessons learnt as Maggie, there is no need to change any of the concepts I learnt in that life, I was on track with that. I am still to learn that I have to realise there is life outside my own little circle. As Maggie I became so involved with my father's business and my home and myself that I felt it was everything. If she had continued in that life she may never have married, she would have been a spinster and looked after her father all her life. She would have eventually taken over the business and never had gone any further.

P: The lady in crimson says that in my current life it's been very hard for me, but I knew it would be this way. I made the choices to make it hard for myself. Most of the life lessons I have set out to learn in my current life I am well on the way to achieving already... and she is also telling me that I'm not with my own soul family because in my current life I had to go to another soul family to learn these particular lessons. My own soul family would never have taught me the lessons that I needed. Edward advised against this, but I would never have learnt these lessons by being with my own soul family.

J: *How do you feel with what they have said to you?*

P: I'm happy that they are pleased with my life as Maggie, and although I know the meeting with this panel is loving it is daunting to confront. I don't know whether I have done the right thing. I like to hope I have but it's sort of like cheques and balances, it can sometimes be a little daunting. As Maggie I have passed the lessons

I needed to learn, as Penny I still have a little ways to go yet, because I have taken on a lot in this life. I have done the best I can to this point and they are nodding, they are in agreement. Now is a time of reflection, more so than action, the action is done and the hard part effectively is finished. Now it will be easier for me to cope with the situations I find myself in because I can use my life experience.

I am happy for her that she understands her lessons now and the guides on the panel are assisting her.

P: The foundations have already been laid and the hard part is over and they are surprised I lasted as long as I have... they wouldn't have been surprised if I had joined them as Penny sooner. I think that's humour, they have humour as they share this with me.

J: *Is there a greater being in this room that is greater than the panel?*

She replied without any hesitation to this question.

P: Yes... at the back of this room, at the top near the roof there is a bright light and the love comes from that light and through the panel. There is a higher being, but not standing in judgement, just emanating the love; it's like a power source for the panel. The love comes through the panel and then through to me and then I send my love back to the panel and it's pretty insignificant compared to what's coming back to me.

J: *What's happening now?*

P: Edward wants to show me and remind me of my selection of my life as Penny. He's saying this is very important because I feel I have been dealt a bad deck. But in fact this was my choice and he would like to show me why I chose to make those selections. He's saying this way it will be easier for me to cope and understand why I made these choices.

J: *Where do you go to view this selection of life?*

P: I have left the panel now; I had to leave formally, I had to back out, I had to leave the panel via the doors, it's respect. I'm in the pre-conception area now with Edward. This place is like a models cat walk and on either side there are video screens.

J: *How do you know when it's time to reincarnate and who tells you?*

P: Edward takes me through lessons so that I can identify what areas of my life I need to work on in the next life. It is through reincarnating that we advance, it doesn't matter how much study we do or how much teaching we do, the only way to learn our life lessons is to reincarnate. I do it begrudgingly, I don't like to reincarnate, there are others who enjoy the challenges that come with a human form, but I don't. I'm not forced to do it, and I don't have to do it, but if I want to advance as a soul I need to do it, it's part of our education.

J: *Can you explain more about this to me?*

P: Once I was in human form in the womb and my soul

was about to come into the body of Penny I realised I had taken on more than I could handle. This is where I started to have doubts. Life selection is the easy part but we have to come to the point where we have to carry it out. This is the point in the womb as a soul I realised the work that was in front of me was going to be a lot harder than I originally had thought. Fortunately, Edward was there with me when I joined my body in the womb. He told me that although I was not going to be loved by my mother there would be others who would care for me. He was with me at times, he doesn't usually do this, but this was a very unusual situation for my soul to experience. Usually after I leave the life selection after the decision has been made to reincarnate I don't usually see Edward again until my death. I just took on more than I thought I could handle in one life time.

J: *Can you tell me more about how you chose a body?*

P: I can choose male or female but I prefer female, I don't reincarnate into male form very often. When I chose a body I chose it because it's based on what I need to learn and what will suite me. Penny has a lot of issues and has chosen a lot of different characteristics. Because of the selections she has made she has been given a body that is very healthy regardless of the skin disorder she has.

J: *What else can you tell me about the process of choosing a body?*

P: The selection of a body is the last choice when choosing the next life unless you are choosing a body with a disability. If you chose a body with a disability you get to try this body, but the lessons aren't really about the body, the lesson could be to learn patience or how it feels when people discriminate against you for how you look. And this could be a life lesson to learn about discrimination, because you may have lived a life where you discriminated against others. If you have chosen a life where you are going to learn discrimination you probably need a broken body to go with it. Or a body that's not whole, because in my incarnation as Penny she needed a strong body because she had to contend with other things. She wouldn't have survived with a broken body as well.

J: *How much soul energy did you bring into the body of Penny?*

P: I brought 70% of my soul energy into Penny's body. In the beginning of my life as Penny this wasn't enough, but now the hard part is over this will be adequate. In times of incredible pain and stress I can tap into this energy, it's like getting a boost of energy and it happens with realising it. There were times in the life as Penny when I was at a point where I could not breathe because the pain and hurt was so bad. I was able to pull on that energy, Penny wasn't able to do this, it was spirit who pulled the energy for her to get her through.

J: *What is your primary mission in life?*

P: My primary mission is as a healer of the heart, as a counsellor someone who gives wise counsel, so I can use compassion. It was not my life purpose to be a scholar or to be a healer of the body; I am a healer of the heart. It was never my intention to do anything but that, because I had chosen such a difficult life I didn't want to burden myself more with career choices and I had to survived. My whole life is exactly as it's meant to be. I see it all now on the screen, I see my childhood, I see my whole life panning out very quickly. My life will slow down from this point, to being more constructive rather than being for survival. The first part was just trying to survive, but with that came the life lessons that I will need from now on. I see now that without the first part of my life I wouldn't be able to do the second part of my life. I understand the skin condition was a choice, Caroline was very vain and Maggie was quite vain as well. They tended to look at a person's outward appearance and they tended to judge how people looked. Now people judge Penny for her outward appearance, this is the karma and was a life choice. The past life I liked the best was Caroline, she was very beautiful, but she was very vain.

This story is very powerful indeed and Penny gained many insights as well as a healing from the 2 sessions. The first session helped her to understand her karmic lessons, and the second session helped to clarify her issues in more detail and to gain understanding of her soul's purpose in life. Below is what she wrote;

The sessions were so helpful; I found major issues from 3 previous lives had collided in this life. Although the lives were very different, the issues were similar. All the guilt that I had carried for so long was in fact not mine to carry. Once I was able to identify this, it was easy to overcome. I now have a completely different way of looking at things; I'm far more laid back. The complexities of some of my relationships now make perfect sense and with understanding comes forgiveness and peace in situations. I can now look back over the last 44 years and see the lessons that were to be learned and hopefully I'm on my way to crossing those life lessons off my list. I now know that the hardest part of my life is behind me and that life now is how it was meant to be. I now have the people in my life who are supposed to be here, I can easily accept their love and am able to love them without fear of rejection. Knowing that you have spent previous lives with loved ones is a pleasant surprise – My brother in this life was my father in a previous life and that explains why he has always had a "Father Concern" for me. It also explains why my husband and I could finish each other's sentences on our first date? I have also been able to verify details that I gave during the session via historical records. For the last 10 years I've suffered severe Rosacea on my face. It was so unsightly and the embarrassment of people staring made me feel self-conscious. I rarely went out in public and tended to socially isolate myself. The pain was also unbearable it was just never ending. Since my sessions it has calmed down to the point that I am able to cover it with makeup and it is unnoticeable. I'm able to use treatment creams now that were just too painful to use in the past. But the biggest change is that the pain has gone completely and that was instant. Without the constant pain the rest is easy. Penny.

16. A SOUL STRUGGLES TO ACCEPT INCARNATION

SUSAN'S STORY

As with all living things, you are here to realise your fullness. Wait not for death to give birth to the vast spirit within you. But death changes nothing more than the flesh that embellishes your face. Hajjar Gibran

Susan was a deeply spiritual, young married woman, who had worked as a professional psychic and tarot card reader for a number of years. Like others in her profession she had studied metaphysics and taken many classes and workshops in psychic development. Despite all of this she felt that she was not progressing in her spiritual work and she felt there was a large block of energy inside of her. She described this energy as being like a big black void that she could not shift no matter what she did.

She had experienced an extremely difficult childhood, having suffered sexual abuse perpetrated by a family member which began at age 3 and continued until the age of 9. During her teenage years in an effort to numb the painful memories from her childhood she began using drugs, nearly dying from an overdose at the age of 18. She told me that she had worked very hard to overcome her past pain by visiting many therapists and healers over the years. Susan was now feeling quite confident that she had put the past behind her. But despite this there was still something not quite right... there was always a sense of disillusionment, frustration, lack of confidence, fear and just plain not being happy with her life.

As a psychic reader she felt a lack of confidence and had a strong fear that she would tell her clients the wrong thing, she just didn't trust her intuition and psychic abilities at all. This block was holding her back... because she was not only a good reader but Susan was a gifted writer. But due to her lack of confidence and the self-doubt in her abilities she felt unable to pursue a writing career even though she had written a book and many poems. Susan brought a list of questions to ask in her session, which included: why was she abused in her childhood?... Why is she here?... Who is she?... What is her next step forward?

We decided to begin the session by working on her feelings of anxiety and self-doubt and to see if we could find out where this came from, maybe from a past life. She went very easily into a deep hypnotic state of relaxation and shortly I began to regress her. I asked her to recall memories beyond her current life, guiding her back to the very beginning, to the source of the feelings of anxiety and self-doubt. Immediately she began to describe that she saw a little wooden cabin or cottage in a forest that looked like it could be England and she went on to say; "That's my house, I'm a little girl sitting in the dirt and there are lots of people around me. I'm in a village and it's all dirty and it's cold, I feel like I'm rocking and swaying at the moment."

As she spoke she became extremely emotional and as I questioned her more deeply she went on to say;

S: I live in the field and my parents live in the house, I look scraggly and the people I came from don't like me. I live in the forest and I heal people.

She became even more emotional, her voice grew louder and she began to cry. I suggested that she could continue to describe

87

what was happening, but if she wanted she could choose to watch it as if it was happening to someone else. These suggestions helped her to relax a little and she continued on with the story.

> S: She is just beautiful. It's so sad, they came and they got her, the ladies came to see her and the kids and animals, but they pulled her away and took her away and they ran and said it wasn't right what she was doing. It was me and my fingers tingle, she was so scared and she didn't know she was doing the wrong thing, she was so frightened. Her parents didn't know how special she was and they killed her. I am angry about that life.

As she died and left the body of the little girl she seemed to take the anger with her from her violent death, she couldn't let the anger go or move on from that life. She kept saying, "I'm still there a bit, still there." Her breathing was rapid and heavy and she seemed very upset.

> S: I did this too many times and it's very quiet up here now.

Her voice softened as she began to have a conversation with her guide called Sarah. Susan's voice changed and the guide Sarah began to speak. "She is very afraid." I suggested that her guide take her to a place of healing to help her to release the fear and trauma of that past life. Then to my surprise she began to sing in a loud shrill voice;

> S: Bring it down Susan, bring your... ah, ah, ah, bring, bring it down, down down... bring... with my tone... now... bring it down with my tone now... bring the tone of your body down now... bring it down with my tone... now... oh... bring it more... you know how... more now... you know how... bring it more... very powerful tones will

come... bring it more... bring it more... you must expand it Susan... you must use your voice with power... and very powerful tones will come

Susan replied to Sarah,

S: Did we talk about this?... I didn't know it would be like this. Laughing she said; I don't come from here apparently, this place is very... very hard to be on, in these funny little weird bodies, yes thank you Sarah, I do appreciate the fact that I was beautiful... I think I made a deal... and what's happening right now is I'm standing right here... here with... with... the lady Lorna and with Sarah... and Susan's body... Susan is having a complete freak out... because I'm in a light... my body is vibrating so fast... that it tingles everywhere... I can feel my body tingle everywhere right now... it's tingling like all mighty... so much.

Laughing again even more loudly she said; Sorry... oh my God... no... ahhhhh...sorry... I can feel it splitting... this is really weird... my body is like not here... my body is here like this right... but it's also over there... with Sarah... totally looking at you... totally saying... Oh wow... God... okay... right... calm down... Sarah said you have got to tell them what you're doing... otherwise this is all pointless... the point is I have a lot of energy in my body... but our bodies are really dense and I need to use my words and tell you that my spiritual body is full of an amazing powerful energy that comes out... but my physical body is just so dense it's hard for this energy to be contained... so I get very traumatised... and the anger... that I still feel which is mixed with my energy... is all mixed up inside me and floating about and I can use very powerful tones in my voice to calm the energy down... but it's really hard to do this on this planet and in this place... but I said I would do it... so they made me pretty... Sarah said that was my deal... they made me pretty... Susan is here to help with the lifting... with the vibrations... she knows... all about the vibrations and the patterns.

Sarah the guide spoke again;

S: Susan is very confused in her body here... we work very hard with Susan. She must move... get out Susan stop sitting on the couch crying... Susan must move herself... laughing... she's very lazy...she's very tired.

Susan replied... "I'm very tired in this place... I'm not happy that I came here... truly I'm not." I asked Sarah to tell me where Susan was originally from; her voice changed again to the voice of Sarah the guide;

S: Susan is from many places, she comes from high places of energy sometimes and sometimes she's from here too... there is a place of energy you call a planet... that is only one place and only one time... and she came from that place... and it is called in your words Pleiades... only from this time though did she come back... Susan wants to play more... she has had many lives... many.

I took the opportunity to ask Sarah why Susan had the experience of being sexually abused and I was surprised with her reply.

S: It is of no consequence... she had this experience other than to remember... to remember there is more than just the physical.

Susan became upset and said; "I'm not sure about this... did I chose to do that?... we forget... this is stupid... stupid... I argue with my guides... because I know these are choices that we make... and I make this choice... but when I'm here I'm angry about this choice... and I am angry that it doesn't make sense to me."

I asked Sarah the guide if Susan could visit with a wise counsel of higher guides whom may help her to understand this; she replied by saying, "Susan stands before her counsel many times...Susan goes to her counsel in her own space... Susan knows this... we won't go to the counsel now... but we will go to the group of other guides."

I asked Susan to describe where they would meet with this group of guides and she said; "It's like in a cloud and Sarah's standing off to the side... and I feel like I have been a naughty girl... she loves me... but she is exasperated with me crying... I'm so sorry... there is something with my leg... a heaviness in my leg."

Susan had mentioned a pain in her leg back when she was experiencing the past life as the little girl in the forest.

S: I'm not calm enough... not calm enough to go any further at this time... there is a male guide there with Sarah... he looks beautiful... he's dark blue and so is Sarah... but she is light blue... my colour is red and around it is silver....and I'm angry right now... and it's like strings... streamers and dots and it's beautiful... laughing... and it waves around... I don't understand there is 2 of everything... 2... me here... me there...

I'm here... them there... I'm so confused... the dark blue male guide is laughing at me... he says this body has many positive things and I forget them... I must express these positive things of the body and then I will be even more happy in this body... I'm very angry though because I'm still here in this body... but I know it was a choice to come... I knew this would not be an easy choice... I have come to bring the beauty back... both the beauty and the pain... both... they say we must learn the balance of the beauty and the pain and the pain from beauty... we must express the beauty from the pain... the pain will bring the beauty.

Sarah the guide; "Susan is angry because she thinks that the people from this planet do not grasp this concept... their history is bleak... she does not have faith... in this planet."

Susan began to cry out in an extremely loud deep voice, "I'm sorrrry... I'm so sorry... shit something stabbed me... I'm confused... ohhhh... she was very... very self-righteous lady... wasn't she a bitch... oh, oh, oh... somebody stabbed her in the heart... somebody stabbed me."

Sarah spoke again, "Susan was very confused when she came here... very, very confused... she had lead an arrogant life... she was very misguided... this is the life not as the child but the life as the arrogant angry one."

Susan began to describe another past life, "Oh I see a nun... she was very nasty... she was the superior... I see the women working very hard and this woman connected to her spirituality but she misconstrued it...

the body... she was a woman who believed in the sin of the body... and she made them suffer the pain... oh my gosh... I don't like looking at her."

I asked the guide Sarah to help her understand the anger she is carrying and what she need to know in order to understand the anger she is carrying is not serving her, it's harming herself.

"Susan thinks the anger is very powerful... she is only experiencing her power truly when she grabs it with her anger... she doesn't believe that she will have an impact on this planet... we feel that she will have this impact... on this planet now."

I asked the guide Sarah if she could help Susan to transform this anger into a positive energy... so that she feels more confident within herself... so she can really help the people on earth... to make a difference... to balance her body... and still connect to her power when she needs to.

Sarah instructed Susan to move towards the light. And Susan described what was happening, "Someone is at my feet reminding me that I must not go... that I must stay... it's a fairy... hehe... a little fairy" ... I must transform it into humour I must laugh... we must laugh... always we must laugh... heheheee."

The guide Sarah spoke again; "Susan you forget... you forget... every time... you forget... every time... every time."

S: Every time I forget... I think I keep telling them I don't want to come back and they keep telling me that I do come back.

I asked Susan what was her soul name, and she replied, "Aya... it means free...that this energy is free to go up and down... Aya... I fly... I fly... and I am very powerful and it must not be forgotten that I can be powerful and be free... I will not be free until I control and understand so that I do not blend to become what it is... it must remain separate... or you will be lost... you are lost again... Aya... I got lost here... I got lost here... in these bodies and this incarnation... I see my energy floating and flying free and I make things and I do things... and I become so focused on those things... it is very confusing... I feel that the vibration is coming back again."

The guide Sarah spoke again, "It will all be alright... it will be easier... now she understand this... she must do her writing and her singing... and be expressive on this planet... her spirit is a very free, expressive and creative spirit... it must be free or this body will be ill... she only understood anger before... she understands anger very well... so she places herself with the anger... this will kill her... we try very hard to shift this anger... she must commit to her spiritual practise and be focused... every day... if she doesn't she will forget very quickly and easily... her energy is very light and it gets very lost... in the patterns."

S: I can feel the waves of energy coming now... I finally feel calmed... they are sending me beams... it's very quiet... the beams of light are getting lighter now and I can see 2 people... a yellow green energy... and a blue... it's beautiful...I can really feel them now... we are standing in a circle... there are white dots in the middle and their hands are like this... and we are all standing together...

there is one here and one here... we pull... now... ha, ha... something happened... so it's like these 2 very powerful lights coming at me and 2 powerful beams... came down at me... sort of bluish yellow... green... like all colours at once... and bright spark on their hands and I put my hands with them and we mentally pulled something... and then it all just stopped... everything's just stopped now... I feel okay and I see shadows of shapes of light... sometimes they get really bright and then dark... and then it's like I have a conversation with them in my head...wow there's a lot of them... I feel really calm and a bit silly... I feel resigned to being in my physical body... I feel I can do it all now... it feels like such a weight of responsibility though.

The guide Sarah spoke again in a very quiet calm and reassuring voice; "She must accept, she must accept and she must publish the book she has already written and publish the poems as well... they will be special to people.... the poems will help people to know they can be in pain but that they are beautiful as well."

I asked Sarah if she would help Susan to have the confidence to publish her book and the poems she had written. "Yes, she will publish them... when Susan feels more confident with her place she will be more embraced with her healing... she will do this when she feels more accepted and recognised for the being that she is... she will not do this for just anybody because it is not for just anyone...it is not safe for just anyone... she must be recognised for the truth of her being... and not persecuted for this... this is why she is cautious... she will find the right path she must know this and stop putting up blocks and barriers... her husband is here to support her... he will stand strong beside her through this life because he did not last time... he fought to save her but he didn't... she doesn't blame him for this... her lives have been very arduous... true spiritual beauty is such a thing to behold... this planet is bereft of this and to show this beauty on this planet one takes a very careful step... beings on this planet are cruel to such a soul... she fears the people of this planet very much... she will attract those who will support her... she will do this."

I asked Susan if she had heard what Sarah had said and she replied in a soft almost crying voice; "I'm sad because I don't want to go back from here... I'm a stubborn soul but I'm going to just let the light shine... it is all we must do really... when your light shines there isn't much else that matters."

L: *How do you feel now Susan...about all you have learnt?*

S: I guess a lot of things make sense now... I do still feel very tired... I think that maybe I won't be coming here again... or at least not for a long time.

This is what Susan had to say about her session:

I feel now that I can accept myself for who I am. I also feel somewhat as if the burden of purpose has gone. I can just live my life, yet paradoxically, I feel more motivated to actually pursue my dreams more actively. I have spoken to a publisher and have an appointment with a graphic designer so I can go ahead and publish my poetry. I finally understand that it won't matter if it is successful or not, or if it is criticised or not... the right people may read it and that is all that matters to me now.

I also wanted to say, it took me a couple of weeks before

I listened to the recordings, and in truth there are parts I find difficult to hear (and I sound really weird... my voice and speech patterns are kind of strange). I almost feel embarrassed by some of it, but I am in such a good place emotionally right now, I don't dwell on it. I realize too, that there was so much that was happening to me that was not vocalised in the recording. It was certainly the most powerful and transformative experience I have ever had. Susan.

17. WITCHCRAFT BURNING

JANET'S STORY

*"Those old hypocrites. They talk about killing witches but the
Good Book's full of magic. Turning the Nile to blood and parting
the Red Sea. What's that if it's not good old-fashioned magic?
Want a little water into wine? No trouble! How about raising
the dead man Lazarus? Just say the word!"*
Clive Barker, *Days of Magic, Nights of War*

Janet is a natural medium and psychic, she described herself as
being able to speak with the dead. She had studied with many
well know spiritual teachers and mentors over the years, but she
always felt she needed to hide her psychic gifts. Part of her felt
that she was not able to speak about her gifts. During a meditation
she saw flashes of herself in a past life where she was accused of
practising witchcraft and was consequently burnt at the stake. Janet
thought this could be the reason she felt blocked about speaking
out about her psychic gifts, and she felt uncomfortable whenever
she was the centre of attention.

Even when she was in a classroom with other like-minded
spiritual students she felt uncomfortable speaking up and described
herself as a closet psychic. In the classroom environment with the
other students she was encouraged to speak up and express herself
but she was unable to because of a weird feeling that held her
back. She related this feeling to a past life where she was fearful

of what the repercussions would be. During a psychic development workshop, she connected to her spirit guide who called himself "The Wizard".

Janet's eldest brother Stephen was killed in a car accident when he was aged 7. She wasn't born when this happened, as a small child she used to say to her Mum she was there when he was hit by the car. She could describe the car and how he was hit on the side of his face by the grill on the car and how she was there. She would point blankly say she was standing in the gutter.

During the mediumship development workshop, she was practising an exercise to introduce and connect to her spirit guides. Her Master guide came through along with others who change all the time and the Master guide brought with him another guide called Thomas. At first Janet couldn't work out who Thomas was. But as the week progressed and she practised this connection Thomas transformed into her brother Stephen who died before she was born and whom she had never met. She was told Stephen was now her guide and was always going to be her guide and they made a contract before she was born that she would be in spirit when he crossed over and that's why she remembered the accident because he would be her guide.

This was a soul agreement they had between them. But she felt confused about this because her spiritual teacher said your current life family cannot be your guides. Janet knew on a deep level he was her guide and they didn't spend their life time together because he lived and died before she was born. She had a problem accepting him as her guide because to her he was her little 7-year-old brother. She also had difficulty accepting Stephen as her Master guide because he shows himself as a 26-year-old man and his soul name is Thomas. The reason for her session was to connect with Thomas and ask him some questions and if possible find out more details about the past life she lived where she felt she was burnt at the stake.

Janet responded to the hypnotic induction well and went

into a very relaxed deep hypnotic state. I gently guided her back in time to a life that would help her to understand herself better in her current life. I began to ask her to describe where she was. She began to speak in a very soft voice and said, "There is a lot of dirt on the ground and I'm under a wooden table". Her face went slightly red, and she began to react emotionally, I placed lots of tissues in her hand. I asked her how old she was and she said she was 6.

L: *What's happening?*

J: I have snuck in.

L: *Have you, are you hiding?*

J: Yes.

L: *So you have snuck in and your hiding... who are you hiding from and who else is with you?*

J: I don't know that I know them, but I know what they do and I think they are making stuff, it's like I'm not supposed to know, but I know... and I know they do it... so I sneak in to watch how they do it, but if they catch me I will be in trouble.

L: *Are you a boy or a girl.*

J: I'm a girl.

L: *Can you tell me more about this, what are they making?*

J: Potions

L: *Do you know what they do with these potions?*

J: Give them to the people

L: *Who are these people making the potions?*

J: 3 women

L: *Are these women related to you?*

J: It doesn't feel like they are, but I know what they are doing, it's a secret. I crawl in from the outside of the building through a hole. It's made of sandstone and it's got a timber roof and dirt on the floor. Their dresses are all the same.

L: *Where do you live?*

J: I live in the village. I don't live in this house I sneak in to watch them, I know what they are doing and it interests me because I know how to do it too. They do it wrong, they measure it in cylinders and I know it's not enough and they give it to the man that's lying on the table and they wait to see what happens but it's wrong. The man dies because they got the dosage wrong. I know how to fix things but I can't tell anyone there.

L: *How do you know how to do this?*

J: I don't know... It's my mum, I watch my mum and she teaches me and I know...and I run through the village because I know what they are doing and they're not right they are doing it all wrong and I know how to do it right.

L: *Can you tell me about your life, where do you live?*

J: In a village... it's like it's hidden, there are lots of other people.

L: *Do you have a father and brothers or sisters?*

J: Yes I have a father but he goes away a lot and I feel I have a brother.

I moved her forward to see if we could find out more about her life.

J: I'm a teenager now... maybe 15... I still live with my mother, but my life is secretive and those ladies watch me they look at me weird and I don't like them. They know I'm scared of them... because they know I know about what they do. And if they caught me they would kill me.

L: *Does your mother know about this?*

Suddenly the scene changed and she said, "They are pulling my mother through the street, the elders of the village have her."

L: *What are they saying about her?*

J: They are saying that she is a witch and she is evil, but she isn't the evil one. And the 3 women stand there watching.

L: *What do they do those women, do they say anything about this?*

J: No but they look at me like they know, they are the evil ones they should be up there not my mum.

L: *What about the elders of the village do they know about what the women have been doing?*

J: No but I do.

L: *What happens to your mother?*

J: They are tying her to a post with her hands behind her and people start gathering because they know what's going on, it's like in the centre of the village.

L: *Where is your father?*

J: I don't know he's not here and I don't feel I need to look for him and it doesn't matter.

L: *What are you saying to yourself as this is happening?*

J: That it's not fair... it's not right because my mum helps people and she makes them better. But they think it's just witchcraft, but it's not because she knows she has the potions right. She knows the correct dosage.

L: *Do you know why they have accused her of this?*

J: They think it's not right that she should help people.

L: *Is there someone in the village they want people to go to other than your mother?*

J: Yes a man, he's part of the people who grabbed her.

I asked her if she recognised this man but she didn't. I also asked her if she recognised the energy of her mother and she said, "It's my mum in this life time." I decided to move her forward to find out what happened to her mother.

J: *It's like she is back with me now. They let her go; they just wanted to scare her.*

L: What's happening now is she still making the potions for the people?

J: *We had to leave, we packed a little bag with our belongings in like a cloth with the corners tied up and we had to run. We are running... they will kill her if they catch her because she can't stop doing what she is doing.*

I took her forward again in that life to a turning point, to find out what happened to them both.

J: I'm in rolling hills with lots of green grass. I'm not sure where I am... there are many tepees.... (surprised) and it's like I'm in another life, that's not where I was.

L: *Let's just focus on this for a moment and find out who you are in this scene?*

J: *I'm a little girl again, with a white dress on and it's different.*

I began to explain to her that she had jumped from one life to another and this can happen in a past life regression. Often they will jump into another life with a theme similar to the first life.

There are a few reasons for this; one may be because they don't want to experience some kind of trauma in the first life so they jump to another life to avoid it. Another reason is their soul wants them to understand a particular lesson and recognise this lesson is also a theme that runs between more than one life. It can be confusing for both the client and the therapist when this happens and it's best to bring them back to the first life and into the scene. I had a feeling she was trying to avoid a trauma and it was important for her to know what happened to herself and her mother in order to heal and let go of any negative residual from that life.

L: *Okay... so let's just drift back to the life where you are the young woman who is running away from the people of the village with her mother... so we can find out what happened to her... and just describe what's happing now.*

J: They are all chasing us (crying) they tie us up and burn us.

I took her out of this scene and disconnected her from her body, I then began asking her more questions about what happened and how she felt.

J: I know they burnt us, but there were others as well. They let us go knowing we would run, to give then an excuse to chase and kill us. To make out to the villagers that we did something wrong and this was proof we were guilty because we were escaping. We were dragged back and we left what we had in the bush.

L: *As you died what were your last thoughts and feelings as you died... what did you take with you?*

J: It was wrong what they did and I'm angry and they don't

understand. We were trying to help people it's just a different way, but it all had to be done this other man's way and this was wrong. If someone hurt themselves instead of trying to heal them he would cut their arm off when you didn't need to. He wasn't educated, he didn't know and the people thought what we did was witchcraft. But we healed many people but they couldn't tell we healed them because it was secret.

L: *Just notice how you feel about this and how you experience the anger...do you hold onto this anger as you leave that life... because they killed you and your mother and blamed you both for something that wasn't true or right?*

J: They didn't even let us explain... but why should we explain, why should we be accused of something when we were only doing good...

L: *What do you say to yourself when you think of how they accused you?*

J: It wasn't fair... who gives them the right...

L: *What decisions do you make about this?*

J: I want to get them back... it's like they weren't ready for me, they didn't understand it. Even if I had the chance to explain they wouldn't have understood, like they had small minds. My mind feels very wide but their minds look like little boxes.

L: *Where you are now can you sense the presence of your mother... because she died with you...?*

J: Yes... it's like I have to look after her, like she is my child, but I don't get that. I always feel like the adult. My mind keeps growing it feels older all the time.

L: *Why do you think you were shown that life time?*

J: Because I keep doing it.

L: *What do you keep doing?*

J: I don't like it when people don't know the real me, they read me wrong.

L: *People presume your something when you're not.*

J: Yes...no one knows who I really am.

L: *Do you keep this you hidden...protecting the real you?*

J: I don't like to be the centre of attention... to be ridiculed or have to explain why I do things... I can't deal with criticism I put a wall up.

L: *How does this affect Janet in her current life?*

J: If I'm not out there they have nothing to criticize me for and I will do what I do in the privacy of my own space.

L: *But being this way... does it serve Janet in any way?*

J: I have to take small steps... test it out it it's to big I will shut down or someone will shut me down.

L: *Like they did to her... they shut that young woman down they burnt her... and she is angry for what they did to her... and time goes really quickly in spirit and all those who were responsible for burning her are here in spirit now... can you see them there in front of you?*

J: There not the same as they were back then... now they hang their heads in shame and they are stuck... which makes me feel good.

L: *What would you like to say to these people who did what they did to you... you can say anything you want to them now... it's okay?*

J: They have gone through their life review and they paid in their own way for what they have done... so why should I be upset about this or say anything else... I'm wasting my time... they know and say they are sorry.

L: *Are you ready to forgive them?*

J: That's big... I can say it but I don't feel it.

L: *Can you forgive yourself for not forgiving them... because you have been hanging on to this so much that it's caused you to shut down... how do you feel?*

J: I feel that they have no idea what they were stopping... I could have helped a lot of people. I was meant to travel, people were waiting for me but I didn't arrive and I let them down they relied on me.

L: *Help me to understand the lessons.*

J: To speak up, don't worry what others people think... and

I do that now but it took a while. I had to do it... didn't feel good but I had to do it quickly so I didn't waste too much time.

L: *Have you had any other lives where you feared speaking up... can you remember that other life they showed you with the tepee?*

J: We were gypsies and we moved around a lot. My nanna taught me to read the tarot for hours and then we would move and I got to sit on the back of the cart, I loved it and it was fun I wasn't scared. I was very good at reading tarot. Everyone laughed and sang.

L: *How did you die in that life... what happened to you?*

J: I don't know.

L: *Just move to the end of that life and tell me what's happening?*

J: (Her voice changed and she sounded quite stressed) ... I'm in bed and I don't think I can get the baby out.

L: *Is there anyone with you?*

J: No... I'm hot and sweaty... everything is spinning, I'm in a tent.

I knew this was a painful death for her, to die in childbirth with the baby stuck and so I decided to take her out of this scene. To let go of the body and to float above it and tell me what happened.

J: The baby got stuck and there was no one there to help.

L: *Why do you think you were shown that life?*

J: Because I was more comfortable with whom I was.

Because Janet was responding well to the session and giving me such great detail which is typical of a somnambulist I decided to ascend her to a higher level to the afterlife. She responded well to my suggestions and she began to describe she was in a library with Roman marble and down the isles there was rows and row and rows of Akashic records.

J: There are people just coming and going but you have to have permission to be there.

L: *And do you have permissions?*

J: *You gave it to me.*

I was rather surprised with her answer... because I was wondering if she needed permission from a spirit guide or friend.

J: They nodded when I went through so they are expecting me.

L: *What happens now where will you go?*

J: I can go to any record and pull it out... it's like a doctors filling cabinet that they would pull out and there's little cards in them.

L: *Do you feel particularly drawn to a cabinet?*

J: No I'm just walking around... just enjoying being here but I have been here before, I like to visit.

L: *What do you like to look at when your there?*

J: Just being in the presence... sometimes I get my records and have a look, I'm more interested in just being here.

L: *I'm just wondering if your guide is close?*

J: I will just go through the back, sometimes he's out there... there is a big table. Yes, Thomas is there and he jumps down and scares me... he gets up to mischief when I'm around. He says I know all this... but you understand it deeper.

L: *Can we ask Thomas what is your life or Soul purpose?*

J: To help people get back on their blue print, that's why I always visit the Akashic records. Because people drift off them and get a little bit lost and I help them get back on track. But I'm not to give them the answers... I'm to help guide them to find the answers themselves.

L: *How does Thomas feel about this work you're doing?*

J: He says I'm spot on and he's really happy with me... he said I will get back into potions but that will just be for fun. I have to do Tarot, because when I first touched Tarot it was like triggering a memory like I knew them. Like memory bubbles from that past life, like they are an old friend. Thomas says I look at potions but I never take the next step, I'm fascinated but I know how powerful it is.

L: *Can we ask Thomas if he has any advice for you about speaking up, how does he feel because you mentioned early you need to take little steps with this?*

J: Protection... he said I won't change my mind, I made a decision to be in the back ground for now until the kids leave school because my biggest fear was them being ridiculed like I was.

L: *So now you understand where this feeling came from.*

J: Yes it all makes sense.

The energy of the session was beginning to fade and I felt she had all she needed and it was time to bring her back.

This is what Janet had to say after her session.

My first life I visited was the life of a witch back in the pre-1600's. I lived with my mother who was a practicing witch and taught me everything about potions, mixing and distributing to heal others. We lived a very recluse life until both were burnt at the stake when I was a pre-teen. My second life I visited was the life of a gypsy girl named 'Lindsay' who was taught the art of Tarot from my grandmother and died whilst giving birth to my first son. Revisiting these lives with such detail, was simply amazing and now piece together much of my life now. I have previously known about these particular 2 past lives but with only snippets of information. To have Lorna take me deeper into the actual living segments of these lives is just priceless - I felt what it was like to live in the moments, relive and view my lives has given me so much understanding of 'who I am' and 'why I do certain things' and 'what blocks me'. All to do with past lives. Thank you, Lorna... you are a truly gifted soul whom I am so grateful to have met you. Thank you for healing my soul, today. Janet.

18. PAIN BUILDS CHARACTER

CAROL'S STORY

"For too long the healing of bodies and the healing of minds have been considered as separate disciplines. The emergence of past life therapy, however, indicates that the holistic approach will again be granted the (respected) status it once enjoyed."
Joel L. Whitton MD PhD *("Life Between Life", 1986)*

Carol, a soft spoken lady in her mid-forties lives in a small town in western Queensland, she travelled for hours to see me at my Brisbane clinic. She had suffered from chronic pain for most of her life. She was desperate to find out why the right side of her body, from her shoulder, hip, knee all the way down to her foot always felt sore, she said it felt like her body had suffered an injury. The discs in her spine often slip out and she had been diagnosed with mild scoliosis and arthritis in her spine. She said she felt the pain only on the right hand side of her body, the left side was fine. This pain was constant and she regularly took strong medication which only eased it slightly. There were some other issues she wanted to know about, but she was just going to keep an open mind and see where the session went.

I was curious as to what these other issues were. When I asked her about them she told me about an event, describing it as a very unusual psychic occurrence. It occurred one morning back in 1996 where she was jolted awake and sat upright in her bed, she looked at the clock to her left and it said 5:38am. As she looked back in front of the bed she saw the images of 2 beings etched into the wall and the curtain. She described this image as an esoteric bright white imprint about an inch thick. Rubbing her eyes in disbelief she thought her imagination was running away with her. But it was still there when she gathered the courage and looked again. As she studied the images she experienced a strong feeling that this was the remnants of an energy that had been in the room, leaving an energetic imprint on the wall. What shocked her most was that she was wide awake when she saw this image.

Getting out of bed to take a closer look she still didn't believe what she was seeing was real, so she went to the bathroom to freshen up, but to her surprise when she came back it was still there and it took about half an hour for it to fade. She was curious to know if there was any more to this that she could find out. She had a feeling that she hadn't been to sleep at all that night, but she had no recollection of anything happening until she sat up in bed so suddenly.

I hypnotised Carol and regressed her back to remember a past life where the pain down her right side may have begun. She began describing a scene in her current life when she was 18. She was riding her palomino pony named Misty, in a paddock and laughing with her friends as they were watching her. She said her friend didn't know how to ride.

C: He has jumped on the back and come on the pony with me but she doesn't like double dinking (an extra person). She is frisky and playing and we are laughing.

L: *Where is this place where you are riding is this where you live?*

C: No... Its where I agist my pony... and there are other people riding their ponies as well.

L: *Tell me what happens next?*

C: Ian is scared, he's on the back behind me on Misty and she's playing up. He jumps off but he has hold of my shirt and he pulls me off the back of the pony and I really hurt my right leg as I hit the ground... (crying) I feel sick... I have really hurt my leg... my friend comes over to help me she holds my leg and tries to straighten it, it's dislocated. It's very bad and I can't walk.

L: *What happens to you now?*

C: I have to get in the car and drive but I can't put any pressure on the brake so I have to use my left leg.

L: *Why do you have to drive?*

C: Ian is with me but he doesn't have a licence so I'm driving home and it's half an hour away a long drive and it's very painful. Mums home and she panics.

At this stage I began to wonder if this was the cause of the pain in her body in her current life and I'm surprised at the answer she gives me.

C: No... It makes the pain I already have worse.

I decide to regress her back further through her memory and I the way I did this was to connect her to the pain in her body more deeply... to notice how the leg feels... the sick feeling... and we begin to follow this pain like a thread back to the cause of the pain in the body.

C: I'm 10 and I'm in Melbourne... I have another pony her

names Caddy and I can't get on her because I'm little and she is funny, I have to climb the fence and sneak on her. She's a good pony and I'm not scared of her but I have this pain in my lower back.

L: *What happens when you ride the pony how does your back feel?*

C: Good... it takes the pain away... I don't know how, my back aches and when I ride it helps it to ease.

I encourage her to get in touch with this ache... she described the feeling as being a cold ache... something's not right... orange colour and a square shape... and I gently guided her further back to the cause of this ache.

L: *Where are you now?*

C: I'm outside in the yard and I'm about 4. I have Rex with me my dog. He's a big Doberman he's lovely and he loves me. I'm not happy... Mum and Dad fight all the time and I go outside to be with Rex.

L: *What happens... go to a turning point in this scene.*

C: Rex knocks me over... he doesn't mean to, he's just playing.

L: *How are you feeling... he knocked you over... you're only a little girl?*

C: He's a big dog and he knocked me over... oh... he knocked me over on my bum.

L: *Before you fell over how did you feel in your body?*

C: No pain... he knocked me on my right side and onto my bum... I'm okay... I give him a pat and he licks my face.

L: *Let's move forward a little in time now and find out what happens to you after you had that fall... do you experience any continuing discomfort from that fall?*

C: I'm back to age 11 now... I start high school and I have to go to school by myself because mums not well, she can't go outside she's scared... agoraphobia... I have to go shopping for her... I feel nervous... and my back is aching and it's a long way to school... I rub it and it's really uncomfortable and I can't sit still... Mum took me to the doctors... I'm 13 now and they don't know what's wrong... they won't tell me... I have to walk at lunch time and they put gel on my back with a warm thing and they massage it... it helps a lot... I have to do that 2 times a week. They don't know what's wrong with my back.

It would seem Carol's physical problems began when her dog pushed her over at age 4. She perhaps damaged her spine in some way in this fall and the damage was aggravated from the 2 other horse falls that followed at age 10 and 18. Remember we reincarnate to learn important lessons through certain experiences in order for our soul to grow. Often the soul will attract the experiences it needs to speed up the soul's learning's. The soul's main aim is for us to experience a wide variety of circumstances that keep us moving back to perfect love. For each of us this journey is very different, unique and not always pleasant.

Now that we have found the original cause of the pain in her current life I began to take her further back to find out if there was a connection to the spinal problems in a past life... because she was now very much in touch with the pain, Carol slipped into a past life memory very easily.

L: *Where are you now?*

C: I'm hanging clothes on a line and I have a thick strong stick under my arm and I'm one handed doing things with my left arm. I'm 38, a female and I'm wearing a long flowing dress and an apron... it's not pretty.

L: *Look around where are you... is this where you live... can you describe this place?*

C: Yes this is where I live... it's a wooden house very small and it's a farm.

L: *Tell me more about you and this stick... why do you have it there?*

C: Its holding me up... it's awkward I don't feel pain but something's wrong with my leg... I can't use my leg.

L: *Do you use the stick to help you to walk?*

C: Yes... it's so hard for me to do anything.

L: *Remembering... how did you get to be like this... what happened to you?*

C: There is a big tree trunk down by the creek it's a fallen tree... it's muddy and wet and I slipped in the mud and jammed under it and can't get myself out... I was going to climb over it but I slipped. How could I do such a stupid thing? Oh... the top of my leg I think I did some nerve damage I don't know. Is gone numb... I can't feel any pain but I get out... I drag myself it's strange I don't feel pain but I drag myself back to the house.

L: *Is there anyone there to help you?*

C: No I live alone.

We have found the cause of the pain in her right leg and side from a past life and I move her forward at this point to find out what happens.

C: I'm outside on the patio at the same house and I'm 63 now... very old. I'm just sitting in the chair. I feel content.

L: *Is there anyone with you.*

C: Yes my grandson he's chopping wood.

I ask her name to connect her more deeply to herself in this life... and I try to find out more about her life.

C: It's Zarah.

L: *Zarah how is your leg now?*

C: I can walk now, I have a limp it's not strong and it's still numb. I'm in America Oklahoma. It's a very hard life and my husband died he got sick. I have a daughter she has moved away but my grandson is here and he is very strong he helps me.

L: *That's good... can you look more closely at your grandson... look into his eyes and tell me does he remind*

*you of anyone... perhaps someone who is in the life
you're currently living as Carol?*

C: Yes he looks a lot like my partner John... he has blue
eyes and that strong brow.

It's quite common to find significant people in our current life turn
up in a past life. This is because they are probably a part of our close
soul family or group and have come to help us to learn important
lessons. I take her to the last day of this life to find out how she died.

C: I'm in bed and my grandson is there holding my hand...
my daughter is there as well and I have a knitted blanket
on me. I'm 72 and still at the same farm house. I'm tired
but I feel happy.

I move her to the point of death... where she takes her last
breath and her soul leaves the physical body. Most people describe
death as being a welcome release especially if they are old or have
been in pain and they are ready to leave.

L: *How do you feel about your death?*

C: I'm outside looking down on the roof.

L: *What thoughts do you die with... what conclusions or
regrets do you make about that life as Zarah?*

C: No regrets... it taught me so much... integrity...
strength... it was character building, a simple life, but
hard life.

I began to ask more questions to find out why she was shown
that life and how it relates to the life she is living as Carol.

C: Character building... yes this life needed that preparation to be strong... I learn, I don't rely on anybody.

L: *When did Carol make this decision that she couldn't rely on anyone... that she had to rely only on herself?*

C: When she was young... dad left when she was 3 and mum had to bring the family up alone and she had to be strong and learn independence from an early age... I missed my Daddy... it was hard. At 10 years old I learnt to accept it and understand that's how it is.

L: *Yes... and Zarah had to learn this too... she was alone?*

C: Yes her husband died and she had to just keep going. Take things as they come.

I asked her if this was a pattern or theme across more than these 2 lives... as Zarah and Carol... was this a pattern where she was learning to be independent and strong.

C: Yes... I think so yes... there was a big gap between the 2 lives... I was somewhere else not here.

I decided to connect Carol to her higher mind or soul mind, this is the part of our soul that is our underlying soul consciousness and is always in spirit. This part is usually willing to answer questions that can help us to understand who we are as a soul and our purpose for reincarnation. This is the part that can also heal on all levels, mental, physical and emotional. She connected easily with this soul part of herself, her voice changed and she began to speak in a very soft all-knowing voice.

C: Her purpose is to show people who they really are. It's

not easy...not everyone is ready to see this... she must just keep going.

L: *Why has she chosen a body with these difficulties?*

C: It's a distraction... she has chosen this body to overcome obstacles no matter what... like a soldier who keeps battling on. Keep focus on the higher perspective. She lets her body distract her and she feels frustrated and out of control... she tries to keep focused but it's difficult for her and time is of the essence but I do what I can to help her.

L: *Can you help her with this to heal the physical body... to ease some of that discomfort. So that she can focus more to help people to see who they are?*

C: Yes we are in the hip now... we are cleaning it out... there is calcification in there... oh feels better... oh... (exhaling) cleansing all the way down the right side removing all inflammation and diseased tissue... oh yes... that's better... realigning the discs much better now... oh... (exhaling) it's flowing like a stream. It feels lighter now... better.

L: *Is there a particular way that she can help people to see the truth?*

C: Yes counselling... not forced, people come and go... drift into my life and I help them... it's good and it makes me happy to show people the truth. I like my work, it's hard sometimes but I'm happy.

L: *I would like to ask the soul self of Carol another question...*

can you tell me who or what she saw in her bedroom all those years ago... let's go back to that time like a movie in the mind before they left... who were they?

C: They left quickly but they came to give me information... I wasn't asleep... they were messengers. I don't know their names they are from another dimension. The messengers are small but the one who speaks is much taller. They say I already know about the universe, the Source and I am to tell people best I can to their level of understanding... to tell them they are not alone and they are loved and cherished... joy, happiness, the people don't know and I need to show them as best I can... it was all planned. I needed to experience Zarah first to be strong because it's not an easy job... I do my best.

L: *Have you lived many lives on Earth?*

C: No... not many on Earth (smiling) most of my lives have been in other realities and dimensions... but I feel like time is running out there is an urgency... and I have to learn to communicate subconsciously with the messengers... I can do this now they no longer need to bring me to them. They tell me I can speak direct to them now. They are with me but there are many... many others I'm not special I'm one of many all doing the same work in different ways... now I know I feel more peaceful. Now I understand why I didn't quite fit and that I can communicate when I need to, they have given me the tools to do this... my best is that I am very right brain oriented I don't live in the left brain much and I'm adjusting my vibration and levels and it's a knowing and it just comes into my mind and it's not me... it's coming from Source... I'm very aware of the difference.

This session was especially special because Carol received a powerful healing and she also found out who the beings were in her bedroom all those years ago. After writing up this session I realized I could have asked her many more questions but time was short. I was really eager to find out if this session had helped Carol with the pain she had experienced. I was really pleased a few months later when I received an email from her letting me know how she had got on since her session with me and below is what she had to say:

Many things have taken place since my Soul Regression Therapy - past life regression consult with Lorna and I'm very happy to say that I got a great deal from my session. Since my session the issues with my lower back and hip have improved immensely and I barely have any pain since so I'm very thankful and grateful for the opportunity to heal. I barely take pain killers now and my pain is now 1/10 and I'm so very... very happy with the results. Whilst I got so much from this experience I would dearly love to have another session sometime in the future as I can see there is so many more questions I have that I know could be answered regarding other issues. I would have liked to go further into the other subject one day. So, to conclude, I am very, very happy with what I got from our session. Thanks so much for all your wonderful work helping people to heal. *~ Carol ~*

19. A NUN'S BETRAYAL

MAY'S STORY

"To look backward for a while is to refresh the eye, to restore it, and to render it more fit for its prime function of looking forward." Margaret Fairless Barber

From the moment May walked into my office I had a feeling she was a little different to most of the clients who I usually see for past life regression. May was a 70-year-old woman. She was dressed very plainly and wasn't wearing any makeup, her hair was naturally grey and cut in a very short, straight, simple style. She looked to me like I would imagine a Nun to look. May told me she had recently been diagnosed with Parkinson's disease. She had a very strong tremor in her right hand and wanted to know why this had happened to her. Parkinson's disease (PD) is a degenerative disorder of the nervous system that affects motor skills and speech. This insidious disease can also effect the sensory reactions, sleep, reaction time, and mood. Although PD can be caused by chemical toxicity, drug abuse, genetic mutation, head trauma, or by other medical disorders, most PD is classified as "idiopathic" (meaning of no known cause). PD has been known since ancient times. It was formally recognized and its symptoms documented in "An Essay on the Shaking Palsy" (1817) by the British physician, James Parkinson.

May believed that if the cause is not known or the effects arise spontaneously, then the origins of the disease could be karmic.

May went on to explain that the medical system says Parkinson's is incurable, but researchers have found that in every case of Parkinson's there is some type of suppressed childhood trauma. She also felt that getting this disease this was a sign or message that she needed to learn something, and she wanted to know what this was. She went on to tell me that her childhood had been very traumatic. Her mother was a paranoid schizophrenic and was very vicious, violent and angry towards her. She had lived in fear of her mother because her reactions to situations were often very unpredictable. May's life was so traumatic that she often wished her mother was dead. Also from the age of 6 until she was 13 her grandfather tried to sexually abuse her. She lived in constant terror, trying to keep out of his grasp, but most of the terror was due to the fear that her mother would find out what was happening. Her grandfather exposed himself to her as well as trying various ways to abuse her.

She learned to cope by withdrawing inside herself to where no one could hurt her and she sensed 2 parts of herself - one outside who could be hurt and traumatized, and one inside who was safe. May had thought her childhood was no longer an issue for her because she had done a lot of therapy on her childhood and thought she had let it go. But when she discovered she had Parkinson's she thought she had better take another look at this. She wanted to know where the trauma first came from. Was it just from her current life with her mother and grandfather, or did it originate from a past life.

May went on to tell me about how she found me. She was staying with her sister, it was late at night, and she couldn't get to sleep. She didn't have a book to read, although usually she had a book with her. She tossed and turned in her bed but just couldn't get to sleep. Over many years she had travelled to ashrams with her sister to see Sai Baba, so she asked Sai Baba to help her to sleep. Instantly the thought popped into her mind that her niece often sleeps in the next room and she's a reader so maybe there would be a book she could read. She went into her niece's room and came across a book by Dr Brian Weiss called Many Lives Many Masters. She took the book into her bedroom, and as she began to read she wondered what was the message in this for her. She had asked for help from her friends in high places, which lead her to find this book, so she decided to run with it and to find out more about past life therapy. The next morning, she told her sister what had happened and her sister suggested an internet search for someone local who does past life regression therapy, and she found me. I believe that May was being guided by her higher soul mind and her spiritual guides to seek help to resolve her childhood issues through a past life regression.

I began to ask more questions about May's life and she told me that she had never been married and she didn't have any children because she had lived in a convent for over 23 years. I wasn't at all surprised when she told me she had been a nun. I had already picked up on this as soon as she walked into my office. May had grown up in a staunch Catholic family and was the eldest of 6 children. At an early age she had the idea to be a missionary when she grew up. At an early age she had the idea that she wanted to be a missionary when she grew up. She was sent to Catholic boarding school and described this as being like bliss because she was finally able to get away from the abuse from her mother.

As May grew older she decided she wanted to become a teacher, but all the teachers she knew were nuns, and becoming a missionary was still in the back of her mind. She had met a lady who had invited her to go to work in New Guinea, so she contacted the missionary order but before she could go they decided she needed to complete her grade 12 schooling. This was a big disappointment to her because she didn't want to hang around for 2 more years at boarding school and she knew her parents didn't have the money to pay for her to stay there. Back then the Queensland government would pay school fees for year 11 and 12 if the student trained as a teacher after spending those 2 years in a Queensland school. By the time she got to the end of year 12 she was really impatient to join a convent.

The Queensland government would allow those 2 years' pay back to be done in a convent school, so she joined a local convent. May looked on joining the convent as an escape, and as an ideal way to fulfil her desire to be of service as a teacher and a nun.

May remained a nun for over 23 years, working as a teacher in convent schools throughout Queensland and eventually became a principal in charge of a school. But suddenly she got the notion to leave. She used to say to herself that as long as she was peaceful, joyful and loving she was in the right place, but she came to realise she no longer felt this way. May became agitated and thought she needed to get out. She talked to a few people about how she felt and they said she was going through a midlife crisis, but one day she spoke to a priest a colleague she had worked with and trusted. He asked her why she had joined the convent and she said she thought she had a calling from God. He wisely replied "couldn't God be calling you again?"

Acting on intuition and advice she decided to leave the convent and went down to Sydney to help her mother. She had read a lot about herbal medicine and decided to study the topic so she could help her mother recover from her mental illness. She was able to support her mother but the herbs couldn't heal her. While she was studying in Sydney she stayed with a local priest and his family, working as a teacher to support herself. Once she graduated she had the idea of buying a bus and travelling to the outback helping people with herbal medicine. She was eventually able to do this with the help from a friend who assisted her raise the money to buy the bus. The only problem was that she wasn't good at charging for her services because she still had the vow of poverty running from her convent days. So she decided to go back into teaching full time and practice as a herbalist part time.

She had never wanted to be married or even thought of this until she reached age 65. But at age 65 she suddenly thought, 'When you are a nun, you kind of disassociate from your body from the waist down, like the genital parts are non-existent, you just switch them off.' She suddenly realised she would never have kids and never be married. She also told me that she had never had any sexual interactions in any way. Around this time, she began to read Mills and Boon romantic books, which she had never had any interest in before.

As her story unfolded I was becoming more and more interested and I asked her if she had ever experienced any other traumas in her life. She told me that when she was in the convent she was elected by the nuns to serve on a general council. But after a few years her mother went off the rails and ran away from home and she decided to take some time off from her teaching duties at the convent to help her family. She applied for 1-year compassionate leave, but shortly before the council meetings were to start the council met and decided because May was not going to be there for the next 12 months she ought not to be part of the council at all and must resign. At the same time this happened one of the council members was going to go to Ireland for 12 months and this was accepted without any penalty. This caused May to feel like she had been kicked in the gut and betrayed, and several of the other nuns who supported her wanted her to contest this decision. But she decided not to cause any problems and she left for 12 months. When she came back she handed in her resignation and left the convent for good. She said that in a sense she felt that what had happened was like they had cut her umbilical cord - it was very gut wrenching. This was the catalyst to her leaving the convent, because the feelings of anxiety and restlessness she felt were the residual emotions from the betrayal she felt from the way the council had treated her.

I could sense May was carrying a karmic pattern of repressing her feelings. Right from being a small child she had been taught this. The Church reinforced this pattern, and taught her to repress her true self, to repress the lovely young woman she was. As a child growing up with an angry, violent mother, she couldn't run to her mother to tell her how she felt because her mother was mentally ill and unavailable to her on all levels. While researching Parkinson's disease May had found a woman in America who had helped many people to get through Parkinson's. This woman was a Meridian Energy healer and found that through working with her patients every one of them, for many different reasons, had experienced a disassociation between their heart and their head.

I began to explain that I would take her back to remember a past life that would help her to understand why she had been born into her current life as May, and to help her to understand why she chose that particular mother. Why did she choose to be a nun for so many years only to be betrayed by the nuns she respected, which caused her to turn away from the church? I also wondered if there was a karmic theme of betrayal, because she was not only betrayed by the nuns who represented the Catholic Church, but also by her mother. She told me as a little kid she used to envy the other kids when they talked about their mums.

I began to see a theme of abuse emerging in her ancestral family and I felt that her mother had also been abused, as well as her grandmother, and this negative theme had been transferred karmically onto May. Somehow she was acting this out in her current life. She had chosen this particular family to help her soul to learn certain lessons so that she wouldn't repeat them again, but until her soul truly knew what these were, she would be stuck and unable to move on. She felt that she needed to keep a barrier up at all times so she wouldn't get hurt. The statement she made around this was, 'I have to be cautious, I have to watch, not to upset people, and I fear being judged'.

I explained that these were the words of her past life character, and this character wasn't very far away. It was just under the surface wanting to be heard. As I began, May drifted into a deep hypnotic state very easily. I regressed her down through her childhood memories and the first stop was at age 12.

L: *Being there now at the age of 12, where are you, are you inside or outside?*

M: In a classroom.

L: *What are you doing in a classroom... are you sitting down or standing up?*

M: Sitting at a desk.

L: *What are you wearing?*

M: School uniform.

L: *What colour is it?*

M: Black pinafore, white blouse.

L: *And how does your hair look... is it short or is it long?*

M: Short.

L: *And look at your desk... do you have anything on the desk, Books?*

M: Book's open, yes.

L: *Looking at the book - what type of book do you have on your desk?*

M: Maths book

L: *It's your Maths book. It's a Maths lesson. Look around at the classroom - do you sit next to somebody... another child ... Who are you sitting next to?*

M: Valerie.

L: *Next to Valerie. Ok. Can you describe Valerie?*

M: She's got a smallish face... she's dressed in a uniform like me... we're good friends.

L: *How do you feel sitting next to your good friend Valerie?*

M: I feel good. I feel good because I'm really quick at Maths.

L: *You're good at Maths. Yes, you like Maths. Look 'round at the classroom now. Is the teacher there?*

M: Yes.

L: *Is it a male?*

M: No, it's a cranky nun.

L: *Ah, it's a nun. She's cranky.*

M: Well she can be.

L: *What do you call her?*

M: Her name's Sister Mary Gabriel.

L: *And how does she look? What is she wearing?*

M: She's got a black veil and black habit... white things 'round her face.

L: *And how do you feel being there in the classroom?*

M: I feel good because I'm so good at Maths.

L: *Good, you're doing well. What else are you aware of... anything else you are noticing?*

M: It's just... she's got a cane in her hand. She bangs it on the desk.

L: *How does that make you feel?*

M: I'm not worried... I know what I can do.

L: *You know that you're ok, you're doing well. What about the children that don't do ok? What happens to them?*

M: I feel sorry for them. Sometimes I show them my work so that they get it right too.

L: *So remembering that time in the classroom, with your friend Valerie... you're helping those others and notice how that feels - to help other people. Does it feel good to help others?*

M: Yes.

L: *You like to do that... so let's detach completely from the time at school, in the classroom... We're going to go further back through your memory now.*

May was an excellent hypnotic subject - she was a somnambulistic and highly visual, describing everything she experienced in great detail. She was also able to connect to her emotions and I was excited as to what we would discover as I guided her further back in time to remember her youngest childhood memory.

L: *Where are you now?*

M: I sort of flitted.

L: *Go with the first thoughts or feelings*

M: There was a hailstorm in Brisbane and I was amazed at the hailstones.

L: *How big are they?*

M: They are half the size of golf balls.

L: *First time you've seen hailstones like that.*

M: Mmmm.

L: *And where are you when you see these hailstones?*

M: At Kedron

L: *Are you at your home, where you live?*

M: No, a relatives' place.

L: *And who owns this place?*

M: Not sure.

L: *Are you just visiting family.*

M: Staying with them for a bit.

L: *Staying with them. And how old are you?*

M: Dunno... little.

L: *Are you walking?*

M: Yes.

L: *And this day of the hailstorm... where are you when you see this hail?*

M: The back veranda.

L: *You're on the back veranda.*

M: Near the top of a long flight of stairs.

L: *Is anyone with you?*

M: Yes, there are others watching it.

L: *Your family?*

M: Mmm.

L: *Is mum there?*

M: Yes... but she's not taking a lot of notice of me.

L: *How do you feel seeing all that?*

M: I'm just amazed.

L: *Amazed, wow. Do they explain to you what it is?*

M: I think so.

L: *Do you feel scared?*

M: No.

L: *Just amazed?*

M: Mmm.

L: *As you stand there, looking out... what are you wearing on this day?*

M: I think it's a white dress.

L: *Do you have anything on your feet?*

M: No.

L: *Is it a hot day... is it cool?*

M: Just comfortable

L: *Just comfortable... so would you be about 2?*

M: 2 or 3.

L: *Noticing what else is happening around you now. Your mum's there... can you describe how she looks.*

M: It's like she's just a bit away from the rest of us.

L: *She's away.*

M: On the veranda.

L: *What's she wearing?*

M: Don't see that clearly but it's just a dress.

L: *As the hailstones fall... do they cover the lawn?*

M: Yes.

At this stage I decide to move the regression on from this time of May being 2 or 3 taking with her the pleasant early memories of that time on the back veranda and move further back to an even earlier time before her birth. This is a time of being inside her mother's womb.

L: *How do you feel being there in the womb, is it comfortable, is it manageable? it's nearly time to be born.*

M: I'm just thinking... this is me?

L: *This is you... and what else are you feeling around?*

M: It's just like I'm really aware of myself.

L: *You're aware of yourself. You're aware that you're there. Are you aware of how you feel being there? Do you feel comfortable?*

M: I'm just a bit surprised that I'm there... that this is me.

L: *Surprised that you're there. So do you hear any sounds... sounds of your mother... her heartbeat, at all?*

M: No.

L: *Are you aware of your mother... her emotion... do you sense your mother?*

M: Only the inside of her womb.

L: *So how do you feel now that you're aware that you're there... you're aware of yourself... how do you feel about your birth... are you looking forward to being born?*

M: No... not... only in the sense that where I am I feel safe.

L: *And tell me... can you tell me more about this need to feel safe? It's very important to you?*

M: It's like it's all I want to feel.

L: *All you want to feel?*

M: It's like I'm... it's the main feeling and I'm content with it.

Here in the womb May is feeling safe, but she also expresses a concern that she needs to stay safe. Most of my clients who I have regressed into the womb describe feeling safe here. Occasionally a client feels scared to be born because they are fearful of the life that is about to happen and this is probably what May is picking up on, her soul already knows what's coming in the life she is about to be born into.

L: *And how do you feel about this body that you've chosen to be born into... because you've chosen to be born... and to come into this physical body your soul's in... how do you feel about the body that you've chosen?*

M: First I was just a bit surprised that I was in it, but it seems to be ok.

L: *What about the brain that your soul's chosen to work through?*

M: Looks pretty big... feels pretty big.

L: *Is that good?*

M: Yes.

L: *A good brain.*

M: Yes.

L: *So what stage of your mother's pregnancy did your soul join with your body.*

M: I guess my awareness that I was me was 3 or 4 months along.

L: *So is this normal for you... do you normally come into a new body around 3 to 4 months?*

M: Yes.

L: *You come in reasonably early.*

M: No, sometimes it's 7 months.

L: *Sometimes it's later. But this time you've come in at 3 to 4... what's the difference then... what are the reasons for you to come in at that time... that stage?*

M: I was anxious to get started.

L: *Oh, ok... anxious to be born.*

M: No... to get started.

L: *To get started... to be in a body?*

M: To be in this life.

L: *To be in this life as May.*

M: Yes.

L: *Do you have any ideas or any feelings about this new life what it will bring?*

M: Just that there's something to be done.

L: *Something to be done. And how do you feel about this something to be done?*

M: I just feel as though it's a job to do, or a task to do.

L: *It's just a job or a task.*

M: It has to be done.

L: *It has to be done... is it important?*

M: It has to be done sometime.

L: *So you've chosen to do it this time.*

M: Yes.

L: *And you were anxious to get started on this task, weren't you?*

M: Yes.

L: *So can you tell me anything about this mother that you've chosen to be born to?*

M: She's precious.

L: *Do you recognise her energy... does she feel familiar?*

M: It's like it's... it's like it's very fearful.

L: *Her energy's fearful?*

M: Sort of, yes... as though she's... kind of like... like you'd see a little wild animal that's beautiful but easily frightened.

L: *Easily scared?*

M: Yes.

L: *So how do you feel about this life that you're about to live with this particular mother that's easily scared?*

M: Just I've got to handle it.

L: *You have to handle it.*

M: Yes.

L: *Ok, you're doing well. Is there anything else that you're aware of that you can tell me about?*

M: I look forward to being with my dad.

L: *You look forward to being with your dad. does his energy feel familiar to you?*

M: There's something... comforting about him... familiar.

L: *Something comforting... ok... It's time to move on now... move away from this time inside your mother's womb.*

May's energy here in this time in the womb was beginning to fade and this is usually indicative of being time to move on to the next stage in the regression. So I began guiding May out of the womb and back further into a past life. We pick up the dialogue as May arrives in the past life.

L: *Just describe to me now... what's happening... where are you now?*

M: It's like an open countryside.

L: *Open countryside?*

M: Green kind of rolling hills... not high.

L: *What else are you noticing there?*

M: I'm by myself.

L: *Do you have anything on your feet. Any footwear?*

M: I think sandals... I'm a strong young male.

L: *Ok... and what are you wearing young man?*

M: Sort of a short sleeved thing and like a short skirt almost. But it's very heavy material... might even be leather.

L: *How would you describe your hair, is it long, short, dark?*

M: Fair... and not really long but a bit above shoulder length.

L: *What are you doing there, are you carrying anything with you?*

M: It might be a long staff. And I'm standing looking out over these hills.

L: *And what are you thinking as you stand there young man?*

M: It's like I'm thinking what now, or what next, or something like that. And then there's a winding kind of roadway in front of me.

L: *And how do you feel, standing there, looking down that road, over the hills... what next? How does that feel?*

M: Just comfortable.

L: *So you're going somewhere new?*

M: Yes.

L: *So where have you come from?*

M: I think the village where I grew up.

L: *You left your village?*

M: Yes.

L: *What made you leave the village?*

M: Need to see what's out there.

L: *Need to see what's out in the world. So is there a place up ahead that you're heading towards?*

M: No, just the long road.

L: *So let's move forward in this life young man... where are you now young man?*

M: I'm at a walled city.

L: *A walled city?*

M: Yes... and inside there are tall spires on some of the buildings.

L: *You're outside looking in?*

M: I'm just at the big gateway that goes in... and I'm about to go forward into this place.

L: *The gate's open?*

M: Yes.

L: *Do you see other people around?*

M: Not yet, no.

L: *Do you know this place?*

M: No, I've never seen it before.

L: *So let's move forward... moving into the city.*

M: It's like a market further on... there are people there, and stalls.

L: *And how do these people look to you?*

M: Medieval... I just buy an apple to eat.

L: *You buy an apple... and what do you use to purchase the apple?*

M: I've got a thing around my waist with a kind of a pouch on it that has money in it.

L: *Can you describe this money?*

M: Coins.

L: *What's it made out of this coin? Silver or gold?*

M: No, it's not gold and it's not silver... so some other sort of metal... maybe bronze sort of.

L: *You have your apple, you're wandering around, where do you go?*

M: I head for one of the buildings, that looks like a church.

L: *Church?*

M: Yes, and I meet somebody that looks like a friar or a monk... and he puts his arm around my shoulder... we move in and then through the side door of the church, out into a sort of monastery.

L: *How do you feel when you've met this man to help you... this monk or priest... friar... how do you feel now?*

M: I feel as though that's where I was headed for.

L: *You were going there?*

M: Yes... and I... join in with the monks.

L: *Does it feel familiar to be with the monks?*

M: Yes, it feels ok... feels as though this is where I'm meant to be.

L: *You're meant to be there... you were heading there. So what happens next, do they give you some place to sleep?*

M: Yes, and I join in the daily routine. There's sort of like a library with writing in it. And there's fields where you go and do some work.

L: *And how would you describe your life, living there, working?*

M: There's a contentment, but there's a... there's a satisfaction in the library and study work... but then there's a hankering for something more... something's missing.

L: *Something's missing. And what do they call you, these monks?*

M: John.

L: *Can I call you John?*

M: Yes.

L: *So tell me John. Tell me about your life John, before you came to the city... you wanted to discover about the world but yet you've come to this monastery... tell me about your life before you were there... what led you here?*

M: There is something that disappointed me back in the village, so I left, to look for... something else.

L: *Go back in your memory John, go back to when you were in the village before.*

M: It was a woman.

L: *A woman, what happened... did she disappoint you, how did that happen?*

M: I thought I could trust her and then I found she turned away from me.

L: *What did you call this woman?*

M: Joan.

L: *Joan... did she betray you?*

M: There's a sort of a feeling of that, yes... but then... there's also a feeling that I mustn't have been good enough if she did.

L: *So what was your relationship with Joan, John?*

M: I think I thought we were going to be a pair.

L: *Did you think you would marry Joan?*

M: Yes.

L: *And what happened... she left you, was there someone, or any other?*

M: She was... she went off to someone else.

L: *She went with someone else. did you know that person?*

M: Yes.

L: *Who was it?*

M: Walter.

L: *Who's Walter?*

M: Just another fellow in the village.

L: *Was he a friend of yours?*

M: Yes.

L: *So she abandoned you... she left you... and you thought you would maybe marry Joan?*

M: Yes, I thought she was mine... I thought she was interested in me, and wanted me, and then she turned away.

L: *So what does this leave you feeling... what does this leave you with?*

M: Hurt, disappointed... and... just wanting to get away.

L: *Yes... and did you have family in the village John?*

M: No... I had an uncle I think.

L: *What happened to your family?*

M: I think they died of some illness, when I was younger.

L: *And an uncle looked after you?*

M: Yes... he's a good man.

L: *He's a good man... so see your uncle... remember your uncle... and the energy with him... does his energy feel familiar to you?*

M: He's like an uncle I have in this life now. He's my father's brother.

L: *Your father's brother... and Joan, who left you feeling hurt and disappointed... see her face, her energy... does she feel familiar to you?*

M: She's dark haired... she's... I can't quite... get her.

L: *But you left. Did you deliberately leave to find this monastery, in this city, did you go there particularly?*

M: No, I just left because I wanted to get away from the hurt and the memory.

L: *And how did uncle feel about you leaving John?*

M: He was sad, but he wasn't against it.

L: *About how old are you?*

M: 18.

L: *So you spend your time with the monks and working... but there's something more that you want?*

M: Yes, there's an underlying sense of something else that I want.

A theme of betrayal of beginning to emerge, as we learn about this story of how John came to live in this medieval village with the monks because he was betrayed by his girlfriend Joan who left him for his friend.

M: It's when I take vows... Final vows and it's like I've... it's like I've committed myself to something and I can't go back on it, but... I wish I wasn't bound to that.

L: *Part of you didn't want to commit?*

M: Generally, the life was good... it suited me, and... people were good... but... in my heart I really wasn't fully in it.

L: *Not fully, not fully committed, connected.*

M: But I took the vows. So I was tied.

L: *You're tied now you've taken these vows yet you're not fully committed. So what feelings are coming up for you?*

M: It's like there's no going back, I just have to live with it now... just have to get on with it... just have to make the most of it... and that's what I do. I achieve things... I'm well revered... but at the same time there's this part of me that's not... my heart's not in it fully.

L: *Just going through the motions?*

M: More or less... but with a certain satisfaction at what I get done.

L: *But there's a part that's still back there with Joan. A part that feels.*

M: Still back there with what I thought I had, yes.

L: *And that part... how's does that part feel?*

M: It's like an ache in my chest... just there (indicates her heart area).

L: *You carry this ache in your chest? Is this in any other areas of the body?*

M: Not that I notice.

L: *So you make a decision just to get on with it?*

M: Yes.

L: *There's part of you that feels you weren't good enough for Joan?*

M: Wow... that's my mum.

L: *She's your mum... her energy?*

M: Being rejected, yes... not good enough.

L: *Not good enough?*

M: Haven't come up to scratch.

L: *And you carry that ache in your chest... I'm not good enough... feel that connection?*

M: Yes.

L: *So going through this life, now you understand this, and how you are carrying this with you.*

At this stage of the regression I guide May to the moment prior to John's death in that past lifetime where we once again pick up the dialogue.

L: *Tell me exactly where you are and what's happening...*

where are you now?

M: I'm on a bed in a monastic cell... surrounded by monks.

L: *How old are you now?*

M: 82

L: *So you stayed with them?*

M: Yes

L: *A long time?*

M: Aware of their caring.

L: *How would you describe your life in the monastery?*

M: Fulfilled in the sense that I've been a good monk.

L: *A good monk... you helped lots of people.*

M: Yes, helped the monastery itself, helped other monks.

L: *You took those vows didn't you... you stuck to them. But yet there's part of you that wanted to do more... but you never did.*

M: No.

L: *As you take that final breath... as you begin to die... you begin to leave and your soul drifts out of that body... what are you thinking as you die?*

M: That I wish that I could've had a soothing of that hurt within me. That I'm happy with myself for leading such a good monastic life... but that I still wish that hurt wasn't there.

L: *You wish the hurt wasn't there.*

M: It's still there.

L: *You took the hurt with you.*

M: Yes.

L: *The feeling of being rejected, not good enough.*

M: Yes... the hurt of that feeling.

L: *The hurt of that feeling... And how did you die - were you sick?*

M: No, I think I was just old.

L: *So you've moved out of that body now... you've died... where are you now. do you see your body below?*

M: It's like I'm in a... sort of, part of a light... and I look down on that body and I'm just very gentle in the way I look at it... and I just drift away from it.

L: *As you look back, become aware of what you're thinking as you leave that life.*

M: It's just the words 'It's done' go through my mind... 'It's done'. And I sort of revisit that moment in the village when I realised I was rejected.

L: *You were rejected by Joan.*

M: Not good enough.

L: *Not good enough... well we could go back down there into that life, go back down there into that village... go back... back in time... back there in that village... knowing what you know now... see Joan... and she rejected you... she ran off with Walter... see Walter... see them there... what would you like to say to them John... what would you say to them now, do you feel able to speak to them?*

M: It's more like I want to talk to me, to myself... or I want someone like my uncle to talk to me and say, 'Just because they've turned away that doesn't say anything about me'.

L: *So you want someone to tell you that you're ok. I understand.*

M: Yes, I want someone to separate the scene so that I don't feel hurt by it.

L: *Because you're carrying that hurt.*

M: Yes.

L: *You've frozen that inside of you... so looking around... is your uncle there... can we call uncle to come and support you?*

M: He's in a workshop.

L: *So let's call him... he can come over to you... or you can go to him... Is there something that you'd like to say to uncle... does he say something to you? Would you like to tell him what happened?*

M: He comes and he just puts his arm around my shoulders. And I'm starting to feel as though... I am... loved by him... and so... I don't have to judge myself by the actions of Joan and Walter... that I can just be me and be an ok person.

L: *You are an ok person... you just ran away from that because it hurt you so... you weren't able to speak up and let them know how they treated you, how it felt to you. You had every right to let them know, but you chose to run away. Sometimes it's good to speak, to let people know how you really feel... you weren't allowed to do that in the monastery... now's the time... you can actually speak and let it go... let them know... if you could say something to them both... to Joan and Walter... what would you say to them... It's ok... you've been carrying this feeling of betrayal... what's behind the feeling of betrayal?... go into that.*

M: Thinking that there's something wrong with me.

L: *Ok... but you know there's nothing wrong with you. Are you angry with the way they treated you?*

M: It hurt more than anything... yes, I guess angry too.

L: *Yes... they treated you badly... she led you on... you thought one thing and she wasn't honest with you... she maybe snuck around... run off with Walter... he was your friend... he ran off with your girl... you have every right to feel the way that you feel. And if you could speak that rage, that anger that you've been storing so deep in your heart... what would you?*

M: I'd roar.

L: *You'd roar... like a lion?*

M: Something like that.

L: *Just imagine you'd have the energy of a lion within you. You'd roar at them, you would... imagine they're there now.*

M: More for the deceit than anything. Not that they fell in love with each other because...

L: *No, that's just how it is... this is about you carrying this energy... so what is it you'd like to say to them... you can say whatever you like... it's ok.*

M: I think I'd tell them 'Get out of my sight'.

L: *That's it ' Get out of my sight'... Do you still carry any of that stuff?*

M: No, I think since my uncle held me I feel much better.

L: *Your uncle loves you... knows you're ok... and you are ok.*

M: He knows who I am... doesn't have to be tied to them.

L: *It's not tied to them at all... no... so how do you feel now?*

M: Lighter.

L: *Lighter, yes.*

M: More integrated... more whole.

L: *So would you like to go back down drifting toward that life where you died in the monastery... have the monks taken good care of your body?*

M: Oh yes.

L: *So it's ok... for you to let go of your body completely now?*

M: Yes.

L: *Do you forgive them for the way that they treated you now, is there anything else lingering?*

M: No.

L: *Let it go?*

M: They are who they are.

L: *They are who they are... they're just humans aren't they. They didn't know any better... that's just how it was... are you ready to forgive yourself for carrying all that stuff through that life?*

M: Bloody hell... what a waste.

L: *What a waste, that life... perhaps there was part of you that hankered for more.*

M: If the hurt wasn't there I probably would have found somebody else.

L: *But then if they had left you it probably would have been the same story. This is something that you have been repeating... a pattern maybe... do you understand this now... how it connects to the current life as May?*

M: Yes.

At this point in the regression I guide May through the Soul Regression Therapy therapeutic process. During this process she connects dozens of lifetimes both male and female containing the theme of hurt and betrayal. May understood the connection between her current life as May and the life as John the monk and how John had carried an ache in his chest from the betrayal and also how this theme and pain had carried through into Mays life with the betrayal from her mother. She described it as a "little gem stone of hurt in all of them". "Raw, sharp, and buried deep". She also needed to know who she was and to appreciate, love, and rejoice in herself.

May discovered that she needed to let love into her life, to allow herself to be liked and to recognise and accept love from others. She learnt that she had been carrying a negative karmic pattern established by those previous lifetimes of not feeling that she was worthy of love, because she was rejected or betrayed by whatever happened in those lives.

She felt it was time to let go of these limiting beliefs and to heal this karmic pattern not only in Mays current life but to heal it across previous incarnations. She then identified the ache/hurt in her current life as like a "big ruby in one hand and the guard on my thoughts would be like a visor on the front of a knight's helmet in my other hand". May connected the symptoms of the Parkinson's to the ruby that she held in her right hand. May previously described her Parkinson's as a dancing right hand. She then let go of the armour that was protecting her mind and the ruby energy releasing it to the universe with love and gratitude acknowledging the opportunity she had to learn this karmic lesson. Also she decided to release all the contracts signed and vows she had taken, vows of poverty, obedience, service and chastity. She saw the contracts being chucked up in the air almost transforming into nothingness as they went. May was now feeling a strong connection of love, instead of the hurt, a feeling of flying free and a connection to her spirit guides. We pick up the session dialogue once again.

L: *You're free aren't you... free to fly in any direction that you choose... and how does the body feel now... how do you feel?*

M: Easy.

L: *Easy, yes... lovely easy feeling... flying free... moving forward easier now each day... easier to move forward... to open up to the energy of love... meeting new people perhaps... doing new things... it's exciting times ahead... that's right. So knowing what you know now as May, what are you going to do differently now to ensure that your life as May moves to a more appropriate course for the development of your soul?*

M: I think my eyes will be more open to the love of people around me, and I'll allow myself to take it on board.

L: *Take it on board.*

M: I think I'll like myself a bit... I think I'll be less serious.

L: *Less serious... have more fun... don't take yourself so seriously.*

M: And I think I'll be in touch with those spirit guides more.

L: *So let's ask them... is there a special way that they want you to connect to them? Is there a special way, now that the communication is open? You've seen them, you've sensed them.*

M: I get the feeling that I just have to think inside my head and they're there.

L: *Think and you'll connect... and they'll help.*

M: Or just have the joy of interacting with them. And I reckon I'll do that often.

L: *You'll do that often.*

M: Yes.

L: *So those 2 parts - May in the past... one on the outside that could be hurt, and the one inside who is safe... how are those 2 parts going now... what's different?*

M: It's like the inside one has swelled up and become one with the outside one.

L: *They've become one?*

M: Yes... because the outside one's no longer just a hard shield.

L: *Right... it's allowing love in now... it feels safe now.*

M: Safe to be me.

L: *Safe to be you. And how does that feel when you say that, safe to be me. You're free.*

M: Powerful was the word that came into my mind.

L: *Powerful... that's awesome, powerful. It's safe to be me. This sounds like your mantra now "Safe to be me". So before we leave is there insights at all?*

M: I think... I think there's been times when my mind has sort of seemed to have shut down... and I've really wanted to be motivated to do stuff I want to do but I've just been shut down... and it almost seems as though now that barrier's gone that I can be clear.

L: *Now you can be clear to do what you want to do. It's about you now. That's right. You've put your life on hold too many times. So the barriers have gone... your mind is open now to the wonderful things that are going to happen to you as you live the rest of your life as May... you have that inner strength... that power... and it's safe to be you... in touch with your guides... they're helping you... you'll have more fun.*

Conclusion

May thought her session was amazing. She was finally able to fully understand where this pain came from, where the ache she had felt in her heart had come from and why. The pain from the past was the same pain John had felt and it was pulling May back. She had also experienced the pain again in her current life with her mother, her grandfather and also from the betrayal of the Catholic Church.

The betrayal in her current life around the Church council was the final straw that broke her back, so to speak. She decided she had had enough and she needed to leave and do something else. She became anxious. This was the beginning of the residual feelings from the past lives surfacing - the energy that was repressed and that she had disconnected from. She had never really wanted to be a nun. There was a strong part of her that always wanted to have a relationship, to have a real life. She ran away from the Church in her current life to feel safe so she could help her mother through herbal medicine, just like John ran away from the village to be a monk. He ran away from the pain of the betrayal from his girlfriend Joan. When May was in the womb, just before she was born as May, she said how important it was for her to feel safe.

She ran away from her mother, away from the trauma and the sexual innuendoes of her grandfather. She felt safe at the Catholic school with the nuns and safe as a nun and teacher. May felt a lot of satisfaction in the convent just like John did in the monastery, but there was a part of her that wasn't fully there, a part of her was yearning for a fulfilling relationship just like John yearned for Joan. She yearned to connect to her true authentic self, to be loved for herself, and, more importantly, to love herself.

When John died he was an old man living in the monastery. At his death he still held onto the pain from the betrayal and he took this pain with him when he died, as along with the many regrets he had. But now May understood what she needed to learn and she had released the pain of the betrayal and the regrets. She was finally free to live the rest of her life in a happy healthy, contented state.

It is well-known that physical trauma such as birth, accidents, violence, rape and surgery, leave psychological scars. Past life regression therapy seems to show that physical symptoms such as May's Parkinson's disease can be a layering of many past life traumas. Research of the Edgar Cayce readings by William McGarey M.D. led to the conclusions that most serious, long-term, degenerative diseases, like Parkinson's disease, are karmic in nature.

Dr Roger Woolger was a leading theorist and practitioner of past life therapy and he also believed that people with these types of diseases had experienced past lives where they consistently suppressed their emotions. This was often an occupational hazard of soldiers suppressing the fear of death, healers suppressing the horror of watching others die from terrible diseases, and so on. When emotions are repressed and not healed, this can create a physical residue within the soul which is then passed from one life to the next until it is understood and cleared fully.

I contacted May 2 years after this session to find out how she was going and she told me that she was sure that every experience in her life has follow-on effects. She said, 'Some play out in my mind for many months after they occur. The session with you was one of these happenings. I think that in this reflective playing out of the events in the regression, I came to a better understanding of my reasons for the way I used to react to things, and this gave me a few laughs at myself. I guess what I am saying is that the session helped me to 'lighten up' and be less judgemental of myself. The Parkinson's diagnosis changed late last year to 'Essential Tremor'. Fortunately, I had not taken any drugs for the former, as it is a totally different health issue. At the moment I am caring for my brother 24/7. He had a serious brain bleed about 12 months ago. This is a full-on occupation for me now."

20. ANGER FREEZES THE NUN'S HEART

CONNIE'S STORY

Holding on to anger is like grasping a hot coal with the intent of throwing it at someone else; you are the one who gets burned. Buddha.

Connie found me by searching on Google for a past life regression therapist in her area. She was a lovely lady in her late 60's, having been a Catholic nun for many years, she left the convent when she was 26. After she left she was married for a short time, but was now divorced with a 33-year-old daughter. She told me she had a heart condition that affected her energy and she needed to take a lot of medication for this condition. She had never experienced hypnosis before. The purpose for this session was to find out why she had the heart condition and to gain some healing if possible. She also wanted to find out what was holding her back from accepting herself. She felt that she was holding onto some type of spiritual block that she described as a fear of letting go and also of allowing things to happen. She wanted her health to improve so that she could do the things she wanted to do. I asked her how her health restricted her and she said, "Energy wise, not being able to walk and do the things I want to do to get myself healthier." Her heart problems developed in 1999, at this time she had chronic fatigue and began to get palpitations whenever she was stressed. She found her life to be very stressful as she was single living her own and felt life was getting her down.

Connie had joined the convent when she was only 16, she wanted to get away from her mother who was extremely critical of her, she felt that she could never do anything right to please her. At age 6 she was almost raped at home in the bathroom by her brother and some other boys who were family friends. One of the boys had his hand over her mouth so she couldn't shout out. Her mother came in just in time and rescued her. Because her mother was so critical and judgmental, she blamed Connie for what happened calling her a slut. This experienced caused her to feel insecure and unloved by her mother. Because of a lack of self-confidence, she developed a fear of getting a job. She thought that becoming a nun would be an easier way for her to leave home and to be looked after. She described her parents as good Catholic's; her dad was involved with the church collecting the donations at the services on a Sundays.

As a postulant and at a very young age of 16 she was sent to Allora and was immediately thrown into teaching year 4 children for half the day and then a music class in the afternoon. She had no training in any of this and was also expected to teach the violin even though she had never played in her life. They gave her half hour introduction to the violin, but after she broke an air loom violin bow they decided she wasn't ready to teach such a delicate instrument, so she taught the children the piano instead. Whilst teaching at the school she met an elderly nun who became her mentor, she described her as being just beautiful and a true lady. Later she was sent to Sydney to complete her teachers training and then she went up to Rockhampton to teach 59 grade 2 and 3 children. She described these years as being the worst of her life because she was under the guidance of an old Irish nun who treated her and all the other young nuns very badly, criticizing them for petty little things. This severe criticism destroyed what was left of Connie's self-esteem and confidence.

She told me she still felt very angry with the church for the way she was treated because of the male domination suffered from the priests. She wasn't allowed to have a voice for many years and it had taken her a long time to finally find the confidence to speak up for herself. Even now she had problems speaking up in certain situations. Connie felt she had been a good teacher but continually lacked any confidence in her abilities. Finally gathering the courage to leave the convent at the age of 27 she decided to make up an excuse. Connie went go to the Arch Bishop and explained that she was finding the vows of chastity difficult to deal with and they allowed her to leave after 11 years in the convent.

Connie married 7 months after leaving the convent, but she soon realised she made a big mistake and should never have married this man. She felt sorry for him because he had experienced a hard life and he was very depressed, but it didn't work out because when he was depressed she would give him a hug and tell him how much she loved him and he would reply by saying "I would like you too if your name was Jane". Jane was his first girlfriend and he had never recovered from the break up from her. His criticism made her feel like her heart had turned to ice.

She realised that she was very young and naive and totally unprepared for a married relationship. For most of her life she had lived in an institution that protected her from the world. She had gone from escaping a critical mother as a young girl, to living under the control of the nuns and priests especially the critical Irish nun, only to leave and marry a man who was depressed, critical and unable to give her the love she so badly craved. I could clearly see there was a pattern emerging in her life, no wonder she had heart problems, she said her heart turned to ice when her husband criticised her. She had fallen pregnant late in life at age 35, but her husband didn't want children because he was adopted and because of this he had experienced a difficult childhood. Connie decided to get pregnant regardless of how he felt.

Even though she had left the church she still felt she had a connection to spirit. The problem was she tended to sabotage herself when it came to listening to her inner guidance or intuition and she wanted to trust in her intuition and to be more open to spirit. I began to see a theme emerging around her heart feeling like ice in Connie's life, a lack of external love and support which in turn led her to feel blocked inside.

Analysing Connie's birth date, her Sun sign is Leo and this sign is ruled by the heart. The heart can often be a problem area for Leos and there is a risk of developing a heart condition if they experience situations of severe stress or serious disputes. She had realised this because she said she had problems of the heart, not heart problems and she had put up barriers to in order to protect her heart. She said it felt like her heart was frozen when she broke up with her husband. There was also a genetic connection in her family, her mother died of a heart attack and her father had a heart condition for most of his life. Her sister had undergone open heart surgery.

Connie was a good subject for hypnotic regression and so she went back in time very easily. We pick up the dialogue of the session now as Connie describes being in her mother's womb.

> L: *Are you uncomfortable, because I imagine it's a little cramped... nearly time to be born... is it manageable in there?*

> C: I'm down the other end... I'm at the beginning.

> L: *Ok... how is that... the beginning... what's that like?*

> C: Fear

> L: *Fear, what is the beginning?*

> C: It's fear that I'm another baby on the way.

L: *You're another baby on the way. So you're feeling fearful, is that what you said?*

C: Yes, because I'm another one.

L: *Because you're going to have another life?*

C: No... I'm another baby... there's another baby coming.

L: *Another baby*

C: I'm another baby coming, it's a worry. She's already lost 2.

L: *Mother's already lost 2?*

C: Had a miscarriage.

C: There's a lot of fear, my mother is very frightened.

C: I feel her fear.

L: *And how does that make you feel about being born?*

C: She doesn't really want to have me. There's too much going on.

L: *Too much going on for her?*

C: Yes. My father's having a breakdown. He's been working all during the war... looking after everyone.

L: *He can't cope?*

C: No... but he's got to cope with that as well.

L: *It's a lot to take on. And she's already lost those babies. Do you understand why she feels like she does?*

C: Yes.

L: *And you're hesitant about being born?*

C: Yes.

L: *But understand now, that's her feeling, it's not yours... that's her life isn't it... that's your mother. Do you see that?*

C: Yes.

L: *Are you able to send her healing energy or support at all, from where you are?*

C: Yes.

L: *Can you do that?*

C: Yes.

L: *How do you do that?*

C: Oh... I just know that she couldn't do anything else at the time... she didn't have the resources, she didn't know how to.

L: *She didn't have much?*

C: No.

L: *And how do you feel about being born?*

C: It's all stuck in my throat. (deep sighing) I just want to be loved. (deep sighing)

L: *And you feel that's not going to happen with this mother?*

C: She'll try.

L: *She'll do her best won't she.*

C: She'll try.

L: *Does she feel familiar, your mother, does her energy feel familiar to you?*

C: No... I don't think so.

L: *Do you have any feelings about this life that's about to happen for you... what are you coming to learn?*

C: I better let go of all this fear that's stuck in my throat at the moment. It's just there.

L: *What is this fear... go into this fear... what is it?*

C: (sighing)

L: *If the fear could speak, what would it say?*

C: I'm not loved.

L: *I'm not loved. Why do you say that... how do you feel?*

C: All in my throat.

L: *It's the throat. I'm not loved. So feeling those feelings... the throat... how does the throat feel?*

C: It's just all there.

L: *Does it feel restricted?*

C: Yes, it's tight.

L: *So going into the feeling... the fear... I'm not loved.*

C: Like barbed wire.

L: *Like barbed wire around the throat.*

C: Just in that one patch.

Because Connie was in touch with her feelings at this point in the womb I decided to use this as an effect bridge to guide her back to a past life where the feelings in her throat, the fear and the feeling of not being wanted or loved began.

L: *Where are you now? Are you inside or outside.*

C: Outside... on a plain... just looking out into the distance.

L: *Look down at your body... connect to your body... be there in your physical body. Are you a male or female?*

C: Male.

L: *And how do you look?*

C: Dark skin.

L: *How old are you? Are you old or young?*

C: Just 20.

L: *You're 20? And what are you wearing.*

C: Sort of a loose garment that goes over your shoulder... I don't know... Sort of a beige colour.

L: *Like a robe?*

C: Yes, but only over one shoulder, not over the other.

L: *What about your hair... how is that?*

C: Short... fuzzy... frizzy... I'm in Africa I think.

L: *Do you carry anything?*

C: A spear.

L: *And what are you thinking as you stand on the plain looking out?*

C: Food.

L: *Food... Are you hungry?*

C: No... just have to get some food.

L: *Looking for food. What type of food do you seek?*

C: A panther.

L: *A panther... do you see one?*

C: No it's a spotty one... whatever they are... leopard.

L: *A leopard... is there one there... are you tracking one?*

C: I think so.

L: *So where have you come from?*

C: Sort of a humpy type of a house... sort of round.

L: *Do you live with other people?*

C: A wife.

L: *You have a wife... and children?*

C: Possibly... possibly one.

L: *How would you describe your life?*

C: Pretty primitive... pretty hard.

I moved her forward in time in this life to a turning point.

C: It's scary... very scary.

L: *What's happening?*

C: Don't know... something's happening.

L: *Where are you... are you still on the plain or somewhere else?*

C: I'm standing somewhere but not there... near my house I think.

L: *You're in your house.*

C: Near it... There are all these others coming.

L: *Do you see them?*

C: I do.

L: *Can you describe these others... how do they look?*

C: Like me but very angry.

L: *Are they all males?*

C: Mostly.

L: *And do they say anything?*

C: They're yelling.

L: *And what do they want?*

C: They want me to join them in war... But I don't want to... I have to but I don't want to.

L: *You have to... so what do you do?*

C: I say no... I don't want to fight.

L: *Do you know who they're fighting?*

C: It's like... I think some white people.

L: *Do you know why they're fighting the white people?*

C: Because they're taking over their lands.

L: *Are they and what will happen if they take over their lands... what will happen to them all?*

C: They're going to get shot... they're all going to get shot.

L: *They're going to get shot by the white people.*

C: Because they're going to take them anyway.

L: *Ok... but they don't want to just give it up do they, so what happened, do you go with them?*

C: No.

L: *So what do they do?*

C: They go.

L: *They leave you?*

C: But I'm very upset about it.

L: *What's the main reason you're upset?*

C: I don't want to fight... I don't believe in fighting... it's why I've moved away.

L: *You moved away from the tribe?*

C: Yes.

L: *What's the reason you're so different to them?*

C: I just don't want to fight. Don't want to kill people.

L: *And how about your wife... how does she feel about this, does she support you?*

C: Yes, but she's worried.

L: *She's worried?*

C: So is my daughter.

L: *It's understandable.*

I decide at this stage to move further along in the life of this African male. The dialogue continues.

C: Don't get much older.

L: *What happens to you?*

C: The white men come. I'm just shot, that's it.

L: *They just shoot you. And your wife and child.*

C: No... just me.

L: *Just you... do you see the ones that do this?*

C: They use a gun... a rifle.

L: *So what happens?*

C: Got me in the neck.

L: *In the neck... your throat?*

C: Yes.

I now move Connie along to the final moments of the African male's lifetime as we continue.

L: *What are you thinking as you're there... after they shoot you?*

C: Rotten things.

L: *Do you feel angry towards them?*

C: Yes, I do.

L: *What will happen with your wife and child? Do you know what will happen?*

C: I don't know... they'll probably rape them or something... do something awful to them... and I can't defend them.

L: *You can't defend them?*

C: No... I couldn't do what I was meant to do... look after them... (crying)

L: *You couldn't look after them. So just be aware of how you are feeling at the point of your death, and how you hang onto those feelings at your death.*

L: *What happened. Do you see your body below... what happened down there?*

C: Yes... my wife and child are just holding onto me.

L: *Your wife... does her energy feel familiar to you... do you recognise her energy?*

C: No... but the child does.

L: *Who's the child?*

C: I think it's my daughter now... I think it's (Beth Lee) I don't know. I think it is.

L: *And what happens to them?*

C: Not good, not good.

L: *Do they pass over as well?*

C: Not for a while... but it's not good.

L: *Just be aware of how you're feeling... you've left that body but you're hanging onto those feelings from that life. What's the main feeling.*

C: It's anger. Anger that people can just take life like that... anger because I didn't want that to happen... that's why we moved away.

L: *But you knew it was inevitable didn't you... part of you knew.*

C: Yes... because they had to destroy.

L: *Is it light or dark?*

C: It's actually white clouds.

L: *How are you feeling now you've left that body?*

C: I still feel... still feel I've actually got the body.

L: *Still feel like you have the body? Do you still feel like you want to go down and protect your family?*

C: Yes... I don't want to go.

L: *You don't want to go?*

C: I don't want to go away from them.

L: *Don't want to leave... so what do you do, do you stay down there for a while?*

C: Yes.

L: *Are you able to communicate with them?*

C: I think with my wife.

L: *She's aware you're around?*

C: Yes... she's angry with me... for leaving her.

L: *She's angry at the situation that's happened?*

C: Yes.

I now move Connie forward a little in the regression while as time moves fast in spirit and the wife and child have joined the African male in spirit. As we continue.

L: *Your wife and child are now there with you in spirit... do you see them there?*

C: Yes.

L: *Reunited with them... together in spirit, is there something you'd like to say to your wife?*

C: I'm just so sorry I left you.

L: *And how does she respond?*

C: She just holds me and hugs me.

L: *She missed you?*

C: Yes... (crying)

L: *But you're all reunited now and your daughter's there too, nothing is ever lost... you are all there together, you're safe... this was just one of many lives... and you know time goes really rapidly in spirit... those white men that did that to you and your family... they're now in spirit... they've come over... I'm just wondering if you could sense them there... do you sense them?*

C: Yes.

L: *You've been carrying that anger towards those people... that could take a life like that... what would you like to say to them now... you're safe... your wife and daughter are there with you... what would you like to say?*

C: You're not worth talking to because you'd never understand... you don't know what love is... you only know hate and power.

L: *Let's ask them if they have something to say back. What do they have to say... if you could speak on their behalf... what would they reply?*

C: That you were nothing anyway.

L: *Ok.*

C: And we enjoyed raping your wife and child.

L: *So they just don't get it do they?*

C: No.

L: *So what would you like them to do?*

C: Just go away... just go away.

At this point I begin therapy bringing in guides to take away the souls of the white antagonists. As the depart they take with them the energy and anger stored in Connie's throat. She begins to feel stronger and knows they are no longer part of her life. As we continue now.

L: *And how do you feel about that now?*

C: Good.

L: *Good?*

C: Stronger.

L: *That's wonderful... So why do you think you were shown that particular lifetime?*

C: Well... to show me that I did know how to love.

L: *You do know how to love?*

C: Yes, I do know how to love.

L: *You do, and you had love.*

C: And to realise that the anger... there was a lot of anger there towards the people who did that to me and my family. To quote something I know... "My heart was made for long strong loving"... and I worry about not being able to look after those I would like to look after better.

L: *So Connie worries that she can't look after certain people?*

C: I am not able to give of who I really am and show that.

L: *So what's holding her back from giving and showing who she really is? Is it this energy she's still hanging onto? Is it anger?*

C: Might be that.

L: *Anything else?*

C: A feeling of helplessness that I couldn't do anything about it.

L: *This is something that the soul of Connie is learning... is working through... to move beyond this anger and these feelings of helplessness... what is this... is there a theme... a pattern... what is this really that Connie is learning?*

C: It has to do with energy... it has to do with allowing myself to live and feel energy... not let what's happened affect me... I've closed off.

L: *Perhaps it's to let go of what's happened in the past... to move on... and to open your heart.*

C: Allow the energy to... this lack of energy that gets to me... to allow that... whatever's holding it back, to move away.

L: *Is it resentment because of what they did?*

C: No it'd be more anger.

L: *Anger... and how does the anger affect Connie, does it serve any purpose?*

C: It sort of makes me want to protect... my friends ... people I know... people I don't know... who've been hurt by the church... especially the abused ones... the ones who've been just ground into the dust by it... I just get so angry about that.

L: *So the anger makes Connie want to protect these people but are you able to protect them, does this anger help you to protect them, what does it do to you?*

C: Most of them I can't protect, but I can... I can't protect them... but I can ... I want to.

L: *So you feel frustrated in a way?*

C: Yes... I want to stop others from hurting these people... my friends... and the ones I don't even know... all these nuns who've hurt people and ground them into the dust... and priests... and all these poor abused people who've never managed to get on with their lives at all, because of what's happened to them... it's so wrong... and I don't have that voice... I want to speak out but I just don't have it in me to speak out.

L: *She doesn't have the voice to speak out... the anger doesn't help to protect anyone... it just harms herself... causes her more anger, detachment and closes her off in her heart... is that the way to go about this, what is it she needs to learn?*

C: No, it's not the way to go about it.

L: *What is it?*

C: It's about letting go... learning to love... allowing myself to love others.

L: *Because everyone's on their own journey... we can never know what's right for someone else.*

C: But we can love them.

L: *We can love them... but while you are hanging onto this anger you're not even able to do that.*

C: That's probably why I can't... probably why I find it difficult to do that.

I then began the Soul Regression Therapy process during which we discover there have been many past lifetimes both male and female in which anger, guilt around not protecting others had been a theme. As we peeled back the layers of these themes across Connie's past life lineage the feeling of aloneness emerged which closed off the heart bringing with it the feeling of not being good enough. Connie saw it was an ever repeating pattern in her current incarnation, she saw the anger, hardened heart and aloneness as a red/orange glowing fire of coals in her chest and decided to release it with the help of her guides, letting it all flow back into the universe.

L: *How does that feel now.*

C: It's alright... I'm just letting them do it... because I just don't have it.

L: *You don't need to do it... they can do it for you... because your guides are there internally supporting you now... So how do you feel about all this now, do you understand this now?*

C: Yes.

L: *If you look around, do you sense or feel anyone else there? is there any guides that may have a message for you?*

C: My angel's there.

L: *And what does your angel want you to know?*

C: It's alright.

L: *It's alright?*

C: I'm just being held.

L: *Feel the beautiful energy from your angel... they love you and they support you.... it's time for yourself now... to allow the energy of the angels to help you.*

C: My mother's there too... and my dad... and my daughter.

L: *Yes, part of our energy is always there in spirit... we only bring a certain percentage into the physical body... so are they part of your soul family?*

C: I think so, yes, they're there.

L: *Do they have a message for you?*

C: That I'm loved.

L: *You're loved.*

C: And my baby girl that I never knew is always with me. She's a happy little soul.

L: *Is that your sister?*

C: My daughter... the one I lost.

L: *The one that you lost... she's there.*

C: She's a very happy little being.

L: *So understanding there's no separation... you're all connected.*

C: She's just telling me she's come back as a good friend of mine... who just contacted me before I came... she's in hospital... she is a beautiful happy soul.

L: *Does your angel have any messages for you now about your health? What do they want you to do to become healthy?*

C: Don't know... just do what I'm doing.

L: *They believe that what you're doing... you're on the right track?*

C: I think so.

L: *You're already doing it.*

C: And when my feet heal that will help.

L: *Are they helping you with the feet?*

C: Well we started working on that a while ago... a few weeks ago... just knowing that I can heal myself.

L: *You can heal yourself.*

C: It's having the energy to keep on believing it... to have the knowing that I can do it... I don't have to go back into that lethargy or that closing off.

L: *Be more open now... allow the healing to take place inside of you... so now that you've connected to your angel and your inner healer... a wise inner healer... within you... is helping you now, to heal... by letting go of all of those old blocks and fears you have cleared the way for the healing to be more powerful.*

C: Yes.

L: *Good... so how do you feel now about all you've learnt?*

C: I just feel more positive... more... well happy I suppose.

L: *Happy... good feeling. Ok... so is there anything else... before we move on?*

C: That... my daughter having come back as somebody else... I can love that... I love that person anyway but I know a deeper love for her... a deeper caring... it's a real gift that is... she's a special lass.

L: *So remembering that wonderful feeling... the connection*

C: Too right.

L: *Perhaps you'll be able to reconnect to your angels easily now that the connection is open... what do they want you to do?*

C: Be aware of them.

L: *And how will they present themselves to you so you can be aware of them?*

C: Just as they are now... almost like a ball of energy.

Conclusion

After Connie left the church she was still carrying a feeling of deep anger towards the church for the way she was treated by the priests and some of the nuns. As a nun she had taken vows of obedience and consequently she was not allowed to defend herself against the criticism and speak her mind about the way she felt. This had caused her self-esteem to suffer and she had shut down on many levels.

We traced this feeling back to the womb before she was born, when she experienced the stuck feeling in her throat and when we pulled back the layers the belief beneath this was "I'm not loved." She just wanted to be loved in this life as Connie but she was born to a mother that withheld love because she had already lost 2 babies and she didn't want another because she was fearful that Connie would die as well. She withheld love to protect herself from losing another baby. But this caused Connie to feel unwanted and unloved at birth, which carried on as a pattern all through her life.

The life as the African warrior was quite short, he moved away from his tribe because they wanted him to fight the white man, he didn't want to fight because he thought this would put his family in danger. But he was eventually killed by the white man. Interestingly he died from a bullet wound to the neck/throat area. At the death he didn't want to leave his family because he wanted to stay to fight to protect them.

After the death in a past life it's easier for the client to reconnect to their soul mind and when I asked Connie why she was shown that particular lifetime she said it was to show her that she did know how to love and that she was also loved by her family.

Connie's soul had held onto the anger the African warrior had felt at his death and she said, "My heart was made for long strong loving"... and "I worry about not being able to look after those I would like to look after better." Her soul had taken on the feelings of helplessness that he couldn't do anything about it.

The lesson was to allow herself to live and feel energy and not to allow the past experiences to affect Connie as they had been. The energy of anger is powerful and Connie had used this energy in the wrong way. The anger was the driving force behind why she felt she needed to protect her friends and people who had been hurt by the church, especially the abused ones. She was torn to wanting to protect them and realising she couldn't because she didn't have a voice to speak out on their behalf. The real lesson was about letting go, learning to love, allowing herself to love others regardless of what has happened to her. We discovered another layer beneath this a feeling of aloneness and not feeling good enough that separated her from others who loved her and this feeling closed her off and shut down her heart.

After she realised this it was easy for her to release these blocks and once this was done Connie was able to connect to her angel who told her that she is loved. She was also able to connect to her miscarried daughter she never knew. She now knows her daughter is always with her and that she is a happy little soul. She realised that she has the power to heal herself, and the way to do this is to believe she can, she doesn't have to go back into that lethargy or that closing off. After the session she said she felt more positive and happy. Connie was able to open up her heart to loving herself and accepting herself more. She found out what was holding her back from accepting herself and she was able to clear the spiritual blocks that she described as fears of letting go and allowing things to happen. When we shut down our feelings to protect ourselves, we also put up a barrier that prevents is from loving ourselves. When we shut down our heart this can cause all sorts of physical problems as Connie had experienced.

Connie wrote to me a couple of years later to let me know how she was going since the session. Below are her words.

"Probably the main thing I would say about the session with you Lorna is that I now understand where some of my anger came from and it just seemed to dissipate after the session. This was certainly one of the reasons I was able to move on further with opening myself up to the possibilities that seemed to come one after another. I think that my session with you was part of the big changes I was able to make. I participated in 2 retreats which were amazingly healing and allowed me to open my heart to love more easily, the need for this showing up in our session. There were so many things that just built on after the session. I allowed myself to be open more to who I am.

21. LESSONS OF PATIENCE

KAYS PAST LIFE TO AFTERLIFE STORY

There is nothing I can tell you that you do not already know.
There is no question that you can ask me that you Yourself
cannot answer.
You have just forgotten.
David Littlewood *(from 'Start to Live')*

Kay was a middle aged lady who was separated from her husband. She came to see me because she wanted to clear the depression she had experienced for many years. Kay doubted herself and felt she needed to clear her thinking. She often wondered if there were any past life issues blocking her from feeling positive about herself and perhaps causing the depression. She wanted to know how to live her life from the perspective of her higher self and to bring in unconditional love, and to live from that place. Kay was a trained hypnotherapist but her lack of self-confidence in her abilities was blocking her from operating a successful business and promoting herself. Because Kay had experienced hypnosis before she quickly went into a very deep state of relaxation and I regressed her easily to a past life. She began describing the opening scene of the past life.

K: I'm outside a building, it's unusual, it feels like there are concrete footpaths around. I'm a boy about age 14, I'm wearing shoes and it looks like I have silver pants on. My hair is light brown and frizzy. There are lots of people moving around.

L: *Where are you going?*

K: I'm going to a library to study engineering. I'm going to school and I'm learning how to build things.

L: *What is your name?*

K: My name is Simon Alexander.

I took Simon forward to the place where he lived to see if we could find out more details of this life.

K: It's an odd shape, like an igloo. I live with my wife and 2 children and I'm aged 28. My wife is nice, she has long black hair and she's slender.

L: *How do you support your family Simon?*

K: I have 2 jobs, I'm working in an odd job and I also make structures, I build things and the year is 1762. My life is comfortable and I travel in my carriage.

I move Simon forward to an important event and he says he is in his "40's now", as we continue

K: I'm working for the company, the Boston Conglomerate, they are an architecture company and too many people take short cuts, they don't do their job properly. My job is the planning and the drawings. I'm 42 and I live far away from where I lived as a boy. I'm in America now with my family. My life is comfortable and I have my own home. I like to make little toys out of wood, and rocking horses.

I took Simon to the last day of this life and he was in bed. He was 67 and was sick with his stomach. He said he became ill quite quickly, so I took him through his death and I asked him how he felt to die.

K: It feels good, I feel much happier now and it's very light around me. I didn't want to leave my family, but I was ready within myself to go.

L: *Are you still close to your body or have you moved away?*

K: I'm a little further away. My family were with me, my wife and children.

L: *Do you have any regrets about that life you lived?*

K: Not speaking out. I kept too much to myself about what was going on at my work and it made me feel like I didn't want to do the job as much even though I liked it.

L: *So is that something you would do differently?*

K: Yes

L: *What else have you learnt from that life?*

K: It was peaceful in a lot of regards although I didn't always see it like that at the time; I was too focused on the work.

L: *Do you recognise your wife, does she feel or look familiar to you maybe her soul is in your life as Kay?*

K: Yes, she reminds me of John.

John was a friend of Kay's; they had a brief relationship before Kay was married. I encouraged Kay's soul to continue to let go of the past life as Simon and to continue to the spirit realms and the afterlife and to describe the journey through the gateway.

K: It's very familiar, it's the place I love to be, it's busy, it's peaceful. It feels like I'm being pulled and my soul family are coming to meet me. They are very light; there are lots of them, probably 70. I'm moving into a big communal centre and my guides are there. There are 5 guides here and one will speak for them all.

L: *What do they have to say about that life you just lived as Simon?*

K: It's okay, I achieved a lot, I didn't realise I had achieved so much because I focused on the little things I did wrong. I had an impact on a lot of people that I helped out. They showed me that life so I would realise that I'm contributing to my life now, even though there are times when I don't think I am. I have learnt a lot more than I realised. I thought I had been sitting on the side lines but I haven't.

L: *How will this help Kay in her current life?*

K: It helps to know that I do contribute a lot, to a lot of people and I do make a difference and I have to acknowledge that for myself. They say trusting, trusting in me. It doesn't matter that other people know more or have more understanding, they don't always. It's the biggest hall mark to trust my intuition.

L: *Is this a lesson your soul has been learning over many lifetimes?*

K: Yes, 8 lifetimes. But my guides say I'm doing well now that I'm coming to understating this more.

L: *What is your guides name or is there a group name?*

K: Yes, Shamarla, this means Knowing.

L: *What is your soul name?*

K: Camilla, this means Peace.

L: *What's happening now, are you ready to be taken somewhere else?*

K: Yes, out into the stars. It's blissful, light, and very beautiful. They are taking me to the office, this is what they call it. Lots of books, rows and rows of books higher than you can see, higher than you can imagine. There are books for me to learn and read about. My guide is there and another person, he's an archivist and he's going to help me find my books.

L: *What particular book does he show you first?*

K: Patience. He says I know a lot of what's in the books already but I don't listen to that; there are lots of books that I have already read. I read them a long time ago, (laughing), he's funny. He's dressed in white and has a beard and is humorous and witty, he's serious but not all the time.

L: *What does he have to say to you about patience?*

K: He says it's not necessary to do it all at once, and it's also not necessary to do everything.

L: *Do you have a sense of what your true purpose is through your lives?*

K: My purpose feels like it's to serve, to be of service.

L: *Can they help you with some advice Camilla, about your current life as Kay, about the modalities you need to learn.*

K: I'm to work with the Masters, to listen to them and sit more and bring them in. Ask them in meditation and in life. I'm to learn Angelic Reiki and this will help me to connect to the Masters and not to worry about anything else right now. This will help me to get more in tune with the guidance. To be more in tune with listening, more in tune with being. Everything will come from that and just branch out and everything will work out fine. The connection will be stronger and the knowledge will be there and help me with my psychic and medium work.

L: *How can Kay bring her healing centre into reality?*

K: Think and it will be, dream it and it will come. It's already there; no need to worry about that, it will be abundant. There will be other learning's, to realise there is no difference between which they are the guides and Masters and anybody else. Once the connection is made between them, it can never be broken. There is an abundance of knowledge of learning the information is all there.

L: *How do you feel about what they have shown you?*

K: I feel excellent.

She eventually left the library and moved to another place that she described as being filled with lots of jewels and different colours and vibration. There were 2 guides waiting for her and she described them as being like 2 but of one, she said "they are masculine and feminine, both but neither."

K: They wear robes, and a medallion around their neck. It's like a 6 pointed star, they are both the same. It means balance, coming together. They are the mother and the father, yet not the mother and father. They say I'm never alone.

L: *How do you look now?*

K: I look very, very different, tall like sunlight but much brighter, very tall. My energy is purple with silver and my symbol is a 6 pointed star made out of platinum, with different coloured jewels. There are yellow jewels and it means connection. They say to trust, listen and remember, trust strengthens everything.

I asked her if she wanted to go anywhere else and she said she wanted to go to a special place of oneness.

K: It feels like silver and much more beautiful to where I was, it feels like harp music, and feels like angels everywhere. There are other souls here but they are more etheric, they are much different. It feels very different here. There are a large, large number of souls here, the spirit state is the first state we go to and then it's this state. Sometimes these souls are separate and sometimes together, but never really separate, just different stages. They are the Source energy and it feels like bliss, being here it's much more joyful and a much stronger connection.

L: *Do you always visit this place when you are home?*

K: Yes, and I will eventually reconnect and stay here.

L: *Have you ever lived in any other dimensions or realities other than earth?*

K: I have not always lived on earth; I have lived in different places that are vastly different, much more knowledge and in tune with the self, there is no going outside other than the self. I came to earth to come back to that listening and to feel the difference of not listening, of not hearing. This is my last life on earth; it's not in my plan. I came to earth to experience different understandings and I have had 17 earth lives.

L: *Can you tell me about the future for earth as a planet?*

K: The earth will be here for a while longer. But not too far into the future, in a short space of time although it may be 500 more years of earth time which is not that greater length of time, it certainly doesn't seem any further than that.

I was very interested in what she had to say about the future of the earth so I continued asking more questions about this.

L: *When the earth is no longer here where will the souls go to?*

K: There is another place, but they won't have the same learning, it's very different. Earth is the only place where you have this learning. You learn differently in other realties and dimensions. Earth is the one place where you learn in this way.

L: *What is the reason earth won't be here?*

K: Peoples knowledge will be different, they will be back to trusting their own selves and they will have evolved. It's to know that you have all the answers.

L: *How do you feel now that you understand this?*

K: More relaxed and at peace.

L: *Is there anything else or any further messages before we come back?*

K: Yes, my Dad and Nan are here. He wants me to trust and rely on myself and laugh more. Nan wants me to feel the confidence I used to have. I need to trust my own guidance and I feel I can do this now.

This session is an excellent and detailed account of Kay's journey through the between life realm and helped Kay to trust her intuition and to feel more confident that she does know a lot. This session also helped to lift her depression. Soul Regression Therapy is more than a spiritual journey. Connecting to spiritual guides and wise elders has a deep and lasting effect on clients who come for these advanced spiritual regression sessions.

22. AMIE THE TEACHER ANGEL

JEAN'S PAST LIFE TO BETWEEN LIFE EXPERIENCE

The wisdom of the ages teaches that each individual,
whether believer or not, good or bad, old or young, sick
or well, rich or poor, has a personal Guardian Angel
with him or her at every moment of life's journey.
                                    Janice T. Connell.

Jean was a mature lady aged 61, she came to see me for a Soul Regression, Between Life session at my Brisbane clinic. She had travelled down from the Sunshine Coast to my Springwood clinic. Jean felt confused about her purpose in life and wanted to find direction. She often received psychic messages and impressions, but lacked the self-confidence to share them with people. She wanted to be more spiritual, but didn't feel good enough to follow this through. She also had a strong fear of drowning and thought she had almost drowned as a child. She thought her brother had held her under the water.

I guided Jean back through her current life as I often do in these types of session using hypnosis. The first stop was at a very young age, she began describing a scene where she was at the beach with her older brother and they were playing with a ball.

J: I see hills and sand, and there is a ball being kicked, I'm in a park. The ball goes down the drain and it's my fault. My brother is angry because we have lost the ball. I'm going to get the ball for him, he's my big brother. Oh... I'm slipping into a creek, it flows to the ocean, it's not real deep, but I go under. I panic and my brother is coming to save me, we lost the ball, but he saved me. I'm not happy; it was very scary because the water was taking me away.

Her voice changed and she began to cry as she realised that she would have drowned in the creek if her brother hadn't pulled her out when he did. I reassured her that she was safe now and she continued on with the story.

J: I was very scared and it was very dark under the water, I was trying to find the ball. In a scared voice she said, we can't tell mum about this. My brother is pulling me out, he's cuddling me now, he's not worried about the ball no more. The balls gone but he's got me. Why don't we have any other balls? We can't tell mum about this, because he's supposed to be looking after me.

Jean was a very receptive subject; she became the small child and spoke to me as if I was actually there with her in the scene. This can happen at times, clients have occasionally asked me who am I and why am I asking them questions. I usually reply that I am a friend and they can talk to me about anything.

L: *Your brother would get into trouble if your parents knew what happened?*

J: Yes, dad would hit him hard. But we didn't tell so he didn't get hit.

During the pre-talk Jean had told me that she had a fear of drowning, but she had no idea where this fear came from. Because she went back to the childhood scene where she nearly drowned I decided to help her to release this fear before we moved on to the past life memories. The fear could have gone back further to a past life, as often it does but is not always necessary to go back further. Healing can be more profound and permanent when the client is directly connected to the event and the emotions related to it as Jean was. I continued guiding her back to remember the time when she was in the womb of her mother and she went there easily.

J: It's noisy in here, I don't know what it is but it's outside, deafening noise, I don't know what's going on outside... It's very tense in here, it's not comfortable.

L: *Can you feel or sense your mother?*

J: She feels upset, I don't know if I should be here. I don't think she's happy. I don't think she can afford to have me and she's getting upset because I'm going to come soon. She doesn't know where the pennies are coming from. It's not that she doesn't want me, it's because she hasn't got enough money. I'm going to be a bit of a burden. I'm going to come out soon but she's just not ready for me. I don't think I was meant to be here yet. She can't afford another one. She's very tired, no time to sit down, she works hard.

L: *Do you have any feelings about why you chose to be born into this life that's about to happen?*

J: I know I'm here to help people, but I think I'm meant to help her first, she needs help. She will teach me, but I'm here to help people. She's going to be my teacher, I have chosen her because she is hard working and will be a good teacher. But I think I'm going to be a burden first and that's how she will teach me.

L: *How do you feel about the body your soul has chosen?*

J: I think I should have been a man, because people respect men more than women and if a man does something he's respected more. I'm here to help people.

L: *Why did you choose to be women?*

J: It's just another lesson, I know people will respect a man more, but I'm to learn this from a woman's point of view and it's not going to be easy, but I'm going to do it and this is why I chose this mother because she's a hard worker and she will help me to learn this.

L: *How do you feel about the brain you have chosen?*

J: The body can't keep up with it, it goes to quick and there's a lot of things to teach out there and there's other things to help, but in this world the body doesn't last long enough so there's a lot to learn. They have told me they will help me and always be there for me, because it's a big challenge. Mums very tired.

The opening scene in the past life was in a school room. She said she was looking in, it's a school and we all have slates.

J: I have had to ring the bell, teacher said now it's time to ring the bell. I'm going inside now I have rung the bell. I'm barefooted, wearing a long dress, not wealthy but very old worldly clothes. Teachers' wearing a bonnet and it has a ribbon around it, she wearing a shawl around her. It's a small school, there's not a lot of people, a lot of books and slates. The men are dressed up; I don't know what era this is.

L: *Look around and tell me what the date is.*

J: Oh... It's 1865... Very old style, we are doing maths and I'm a little boy about 12 years of age, I'm called Charlie Hammer. I'm a big boy for my age, that's why I ring the bell. My teacher is called Miss Reaves. I don't like school, I like to go outside. The teacher is wearing a big frilly dress and a girl in the class has pigtails. They wear these funny bonnets.

I moved Charlie forward in time to the place where he lived with his family and he describes a scene where they are having dinner.

J: It's like English style farmhouse, we have lots of land and I'm looking outside and there's lots of green, green grass. Big willow trees, I'm in England. I'm an English boy and our table is big, wooden with hard backed chairs. I have 2 brothers and a sister, mum and dad are sitting at the table. There's a big wood stove and a big fireplace. My dad's name is Harry. Dad is a blacksmith, he works on this farm. There is a big house and mum works there as a maid. They are good to us, but we don't live there, we live here in this farmhouse. Their name is Pettigrew and we are not allowed to go over there.

I moved Charlie forward again and he said he was horse riding and the horse tripped and fell.

J: I hit my head on a rock. I'm about 16, the horse just bolted and I'm watching people looking at me. They have come to help me and I have died and I'm looking down and I can see mum and dad, they are very upset. They bring this old wagon and put my body into it, mums so upset, she says he's too young. I'm okay, but mums really upset. I think I lived in Chestershire, I can't spell. They call me dummy, but that's okay.

L: *What did you learn from that life?*

J: I learnt that some people are rich and some are poor, but we are really all the same. Mum and Dad taught us this.

L: *What happens now?*

J: I can look down, but I have no connection and I can see people are sad, but I'm not sad, I'm looking forward to meeting my friends. I can see them they are just like me and we are floating together. It's very clear and there is a lot of purple around and there is a presence there. I'm going up to that person. It feels so peaceful so lovely to be home, the warmth it's so beautiful, this is a safe place. He's my guardian angel Michael, we have met before and he tells me he's been watching over me. He wants me to go with him, but I don't want to go just yet. This is my home, I'm floating around and it smells so pure, you just wouldn't want to leave here, can you smell them? He's just like us, he's a soul in spirit, and he's brilliant white with a purple aura around him that's why he stands out. I don't have that yet, I'm just blue.

Charlie's life was short; he died tragically in the horse riding accident at age 16. He was ready to leave his family and move on to the between life once he realised he had died. This is common, most souls are ready to move on once they realise they are dead. It was interesting to note that this client was speaking to me as if I was actually there with her soul experiencing what she was experiencing, when Jean asked me if I could smell the pure smells of the spirit world. I view this as being evidence that she was fully connected to her soul energy.

J: I have to go now, they have told me they are very proud of what I did in that life as Charlie. I didn't fulfil what I was supposed to be there for. I was supposed to help people and I didn't do it.

L: *How were you to help them?*

J: I was to become a teacher. Not a teacher as such, but a teacher to build boats. I was supposed to be a teacher to help people to build boasts as a means of travel. A teacher in a sense but it was hands on, but I didn't do that.

L: *The accident Charlie had on the horse that caused his death, did you plan to die that young?*

J: I didn't want to be a builder, my guides told me I was a clever person and I could be a builder, but I didn't want to do that when I got to earth. I'm not a good scholar, so I came home. They knew, but they are not angry and are very understanding and help me to choose another life and another learning lesson.

L: *What is your immortal soul name?*

J: You will laugh, it's Amie, it's not a girl's name or a boy's name and we all get different names, it's an angel name. There are so many angels, people have no idea how many are here. We all know one another because really we are all connected. We all come down to help people to learn.

L: *Do you prefer to reincarnate as a male or female?*

J: No mainly as a female. This is where Charlie went wrong, because I watched other souls go down to earth and I thought they were more respected as men. I thought I would try it as a male, but I was no good at it. Michael says I'm a very good strong person and teacher and I have to keep coming back to learn this, but I guess I'm not a very good pupil. As Jean he's trying to help me and to help me understand. Sometimes there is a long gap between lives; there is no time span as there is on earth. We don't see it like earth or compare it to earth. But if I was to compare it to earth years it would be at least 100 years, but most people don't come back straight away. To come back straight away they would have to be really smart ones, at a higher level. They know how to do things they are the clever ones. I'm being taken to a special meeting now.

L: *How do you get there?*

J: I'm sitting on these seats; there are others here as well. It's not formation like earth, seats but not real seats. The gate is opening now so we are going inside. I don't know how to describe it; I have been here before but I can't remember. It's like a place as a church but not solid and now we are going up.

L: *Can you describe how they look, are they sitting or standing?*

J: Oh no they are sitting, and they have a big book with a gold rim around it. They are going through the things I have done; they are not happy with me coming back so early. Their plan was for me to be a teacher to build boats, because people will start travelling on boats. It will be a new way of the world.

I decided to do some research into this, convict ships began transporting people to Australia around 1787-1868 and the United Kingdom had assisted passage schemes for people wanting to immigrate to Australia from 1847-1886. This would tie in with this information because Charlie was 12 years of age in 1865 and if he had lived to become a boat builder and teacher this fits in well with the period in history when the boat became the way of mass transportation between countries.

J: There are 7 angels here, they are just energy, but we know who we are. Their names are Ariel, Michael, and Abraham I don't know who the others are. Michael is my main guide and he is with me. He's like a specialist teacher down on earth for me.

I took this opportunity to ask the questions Jean had brought with her for the session. I address Jean as Amie now because this is her soul name.

L: *Amie, Jean wants to know what her main lessons are and why she chose her current life.*

J: She has to listen, and do what's she's told. We have to teach her that she is good, but she won't listen. Michael gets very weary because he sends so many messages to her, but it doesn't prove anything to her. Her main lesson is to listen, to listen to everybody and then teach. She has a good heart and there are a lot of bad people, she's a kind person. What we want her to do if she would listen is to teach about us, about spirit. If she listens and passes messages on, then she can help us to connect. People need to know about us, that we are here for them. We want to channel with her, but she doesn't listen she lacks so much confidence. Up here she believes and understands who she is, but when she is down there on the earth in a human body she forgets. We tried to teach her when she was Charlie, to teach him how to build the boats but he wouldn't listen and so Charlie died. She is a very spiritual person and she has been to earth many, many times, but she can't advance until she learns this lesson. This is her final lesson. Then she won't need to come back to earth again and she will be an angel, but she can't be an angel until she learns this.

She suddenly switched back to speaking as the personality of Charlie complaining he had a pain in the head from the fall off the Horse. This often happens during sessions such as these. I asked the soul of Charlie if he would like to move to a healing chamber or place to heal and restore his energies from that past life and he said yes.

J: Michael says he's going to really help me next time and the pains gone now and we are going to an area where there are a lot of people. We kind of all know each other; we don't wear clothes like when I'm on the ground. We are in a spirit form; some forms of spirits don't make it up here. Sometimes people die a bad death and the spirit is troubled and they don't want to come up. They try to hang around their loved ones because they are tormented. My friend Tom, he's still down there with his body and his family. This is where we talk now; we talk about our work and our guides and our friends. But Tom should have been here, but he didn't make it.

L: *Who is Tom?*

J: He's another member of our group. We are all part of this group that come and go, we are born and go and then come back together. Sometimes we might miss each other. Our group guide is Michael.

L: *Are you all at the same soul level as each other?*

J: We are all at different levels, but we all understand and learn from each other. I'm supposed to be helping the newer ones. This is part of the training for my next stage. But I like this stage, this stage you don't have to be responsible. But Michael is responsible for all of us. We all connect up, but we don't remember when we get to earth. All our soul names begin with A's.

L: *Do you recognise anyone who is in the life you're living as Jean?*

J: Yes I see Claude and Paul is here. This is my entire group, my family group. There are 5, but 3 are not from my current life, they are from another life. Claude comes forward, he's very high up. He says I'm a silly thing. He's impatient because he knows I have the ability to be at a higher level. They are a bit serious and I just want to have fun.

L: *What do you do to have fun?*

J: We just watch everyone, to see what's going on. Some are naughty spirits, people on earth call them ghosts but they're not ghosts. They are just spirits playing and having fun and we can do that but people on earth get frightened. But then the funny thing is we are all spirits and when we go back down we forget. We forget we are playing with our friends because they are in body and we are in spirit. When we are in body we forget our spirit friends, and we get a fright. That's when it's good fun.

L: *What percentage of energy did you bring with you into Jeans life?*

J: Well this is the last time I will come back, I'm going to get it right this time and I have enough energy to do it. I love my life as Jean, and I'm comfortable with that. I have to get my act together; Michael is just saying this to me now. It's the time in my life to do it now. I just need to take notice of what's given to me and implement it and spread the word. I need to believe in myself and in my psychic abilities. I'm here to help the spirit world.

After this session Jean felt very happy with what she had learnt. I asked her how she felt about going swimming and she said she now felt very confident and looked forward to it. She also realised she needed to join a spiritual group and seek guidance to help her with her psychic work. She believed this would help her to feel more confident to use her psychic gifts. She was also pleased to have connected to her spirit guide Michael and intended to listen more careful to him through meditation in the future.

23. GENDER MAKES NO SENSE

CHRISTINE'S PAST LIFE TO BETWEEN LIFE EXPERIENCE

Souls don't have genders; we are here to learn, to grow wise, and to love. Dr Brian Weiss

Christine was a vibrant and attractive gay woman aged 44. She came to me for a Soul Regression between life session; this is a more advanced session than a past life regression. The client is guided to look at a past life memory, often the last life they have lived before the current life and then once they soul leaves to body in the past life they are guided to cross over to the between life. This is the place where all souls return between incarnations, between various life times. The place where the soul can rest, heal from a traumatic past life and eventually chose the next life and the lessons they want to experience. Often they connect to their soul family members and spiritual guides.

Christine came in with some questions as most of my clients do. She wanted to understand her soul contract with her partner Jordan. Jordan believed that Christine was her spiritual guide and they wanted confirmation about this either way if possible. She had questions about her family; she wanted to know if they were in her soul family. One of the main aspect of past life regression therapy involves identifying people in the past lives from the client's current lifetime. The recognition of the same souls in different lifetimes has many benefits for a person's healing and transformation. Another benefit of this is that the client can gain a better understanding of current life relationship dynamics.

She was curious to know if she had lived lives on any other planets or realms as another life form. She also wanted to know why she chose to be a gay woman in this lifetime. Christine had experienced a type of sleep paralysis that she couldn't control and this worried her, so she wanted to know if she could get any information about this condition.

The opening scene in the past life memory was in a sandy desert. Christine described herself as a young boy around 15 years of age. Sitting in a small mud building with his mother and brothers, he was wondering how he could help his mother feed the family. As Christine went deeper into the story, she easily began to describe more details.

C: I'm wearing a type of tunic with a gold belt around my middle, my skin is olive, and I have dark curly hair. I have been given a pot by my mother to go and to collect something, and I can see all these men running and I'm really scared. I reluctantly join the crowd and run, but I don't know what they are doing. I think they are going to get grain, I'm only 15 and I have to run with all these big strong men and I don't feel strong enough. I start running with them, carrying the pot, I'm running towards a building that looks like a pyramid shaped temple, but it's got a hole in the bottom, grain is pouring out of the hole. Everyone is filling up their pots and I can't get in front and everyone is stepping over each other, they are all so desperate. I don't know if I make it, I feel trampled on.

L: *Do you have a father?*

C: No my father is not there. He's working somewhere else, he's a soldier and I'm the eldest boy. My name is Elijah and I live in Mesopotamia.

I did some research into Mesopotamia and discovered the name comes from a Greek word, meaning 'between 2 rivers', and was an ancient area in the eastern Mediterranean in the region of Sumer, in the 4th millennium, BCE. Bounded in the northeast by the Zagros Mountains and in the southeast by the Arabian Plateau, corresponding to today's Iraq, mostly, but also parts of modern-day Iran, Syria and Turkey. Unlike the more unified civilizations of Egypt or Greece, Mesopotamia was a collection of varied cultures whose only real bonds were their script, their gods, and their attitude toward women. Women enjoyed nearly equal rights and could own land, file for divorce, own their own businesses, and make contracts in trade.

Mesopotamia is known as the "cradle of civilization" primarily because of 2 developments that occurred there. The invention of the wheel is credited to the Mesopotamians and, in 1922 CE, the archaeologist Sir Leonard Woolley discovered "the remains of 2, 4-wheeled wagons, at the site of the ancient city of Ur, this is the oldest wheeled vehicles in history ever found. Other important developments or inventions credited to the Mesopotamians include the domestication of animals, agriculture, common tools, sophisticated weaponry and warfare, the chariot, wine, beer, demarcation of time into hours, minutes, and seconds, religious rites, the sail (sailboats), and irrigation.

L: *Tell me more about your life and your mother.*

C: I recognise my mother; she feels like my mother in my current life. She has a veil over her head and she sitting on the ground in a dirt building with the other children. I have a sister about 12 and there are 2 other babies, brothers. My mother has a lot of faith in me, we won't have another opportunity to get the grain. Someone's been storing the grain and they shouldn't have been hording it. They should have been feeding us. She said it's the priests who guard the temple and it's wrong. I must help her, but I'm very scared. I'm running now and the pots really heavy and I'm not very big for my age and everyone towers over me yelling and screaming. It's wild and crazy and I get swallowed up in the crowd and I'm knocked to the ground and everything goes black.

This seemed like the death scene, so I moved him forward to see what happened.

C: I see my body there, but I'm not in it. I don't feel any remorse or pain, it's actually okay. He did what he had to do. There is like an indigo blue light pulling me up, it's a very gentle soft feeling. Everything's really bright, it feels familiar. I'm alone and I feel like I'm home. I'm in an area of white light, bright light, just peace and joy all around me and I feel this is where I really belong, this is home. I'm absorbing the surroundings and being part of the oneness again. I'm getting a bit of a charge before I go.

Often when a soul dies in a traumatic way the first place of call in the between life is a resting place or healing chamber. This is a spirit place where the soul can rest and restore themselves before they connect on to meet with their soul family or spiritual guide. I encouraged Christine's soul to soak up the energy of this place and to cleanse her soul from the past life. When they die violently or suddenly don't know they have died they can become confused. Often a spiritual helper will explain to them what happened and where they need to go next. As we continue this is what happens to Christine; she receives a telepathic message where to go next.

C: Now I'm being told to go down a corridor, but I'm still alone. I go down, it's not really like walking, and at the end is a chamber filled with light. It's like the light is a white floor and radiates up the walls, it's not really a room and the colours change as they go up the walls. Looks like people sitting around in a circle, beings, not people. I join the circle and join in with the energy, it's like I'm one of them. This is my soul family, no hierarchy; there was a place for me, a gap I had to fill. I'm representative of them on earth. They don't all chose to go to earth; it's like I chose these assignments for the experience and bring back information so we can all learn.

L: *Do you recognise anyone in this group from your current life?*

C: Yes, my grandmother is in the group, my uncle Ashley and my dad. My dad has a really high place, because he emanates the most love. There are about 6 of us. My dad is pure blue energy, my grandmother is half blue and purple and my uncle is pure blue. My energy is blue with purple mixed in.

L: *Do they have any messages for you? And what do they think about the past life you lived as Elijah?*

C: They said Elijah did the right thing and it was what he was meant to do. This life is about putting me before others because I have never done it before. Always got myself killed helping others. The purple energy keeps washing through me with the blue, they are bathing me in the light and it feels wonderful.

L: *Can you describe how they all look?*

C: My father is wearing a medallion, a 5 pointed star with jewels embedded into it, it symbolises his state of joy, a state of oneness with the universe and all that is. My uncle is wearing a triangle with a circle in the middle, this represents being grounded and reaching and being in touch with the other realms which is represented by the circle. My grandmother is wearing a symbol with squiggly lines, symbolic of the shapes of the universe. We help others the 6 of us; they are there to help the others. One is Anna my friend, she is purple and pink. Jordan is there, her aura doesn't make any sense it's a reddish brown, she's there for the learning and absorbs our energy and she's chosen some tough lives.

L: *Who do you reincarnate with the most?*

C: My father and Jordan. My father is my guide and Jordan is my spiritual partner, it doesn't matter what gender we encounter. Feels like half of the lives I have lived have been with her, but my father is in every life and sometimes he reincarnates as woman.

L: *What is the level of soul advancement of you group?*

C: Some are advancing more rapidly than others, I'm advancing at a medium rate at the moment because I have chosen some lives that have been very difficult, so I have had to slow down. My current life is about learning and also meant to be easy so I understand the learning and helping Jordan with her quest. She has chosen to advance at a very high rate. So one of us must be with her for the rest of this life and that's me.

L: *Why have you chosen to come into a female body in the life as Christine?*

C: I can't get used to the fact that there is gender; it makes no sense to me. My father is also genderless as well, he says to me it doesn't matter. Jordan isn't there as a soul family member she's like an exchange student, she's from another group. She's there for challenges, but she can't face them alone. Our group is expansive and we work on many other plans besides the earthly one. We have lived in many other dimensions, not planets dimensions. They still exist and are not as restrictive as earth; earth is very restrictive that's why you get the most learning from here. Sometimes I have a body and sometimes I'm in energy form. There is a world where I'm crawling on the ground, but I'm an intelligent being and I don't live on the land, I live in the water and the energy around is very soft. When I go back to this place I'm bathed in a pink liquid to absorb all the learning. I learnt independence, because on that world you're alone and you don't require others around you to procreate, you're actually alone.

L: *Why did you choose to reincarnate on earth?*

C: I decided to come to earth because my physical form was uncomfortable there... of crawling. I was like a snail like creature and it was uncomfortable and I have had visitations from these creatures in my life as Christine. They are just beautiful creatures, the softest and gentlest.

L: *What are your lessons in your current life?*

C: My current life is the most significant life because I don't get killed and I need to look after my body to make sure I don't leave early... this is the learning. This is why I'm female in this life so I don't take to many risks, I have died many times taking risks as a male. Jordan requested I come back as a female in this life; otherwise she would have lost me, because I would have been reckless. I'm more cautious as a female. Jordan requested that I reincarnate, but there was some resistance. Eventually I realised this was okay because we would both get something out of it.

L: *Do you have many choices in the type of lives that are available for you to choose?*

C: Yes, I had 2 choices, the life as Corrie and another life as a soldier. He would have been killed; his name was Jason Cooper, I'm not sure if any other soul came in for him. The life was in England and he would have fought in one of the wars, in a jungle and he would have been born on the same day I was born as Christine . This life is the longer life.

L: *How do you choose your lives, what's the process?*

C: It's like a movie theatre, like a 3D Imax theatre. We see it larger than life; we see the entirety of the life. I have seen the entirety of this life and Jason's life. Higher beings help us to choose the best life with the most learning. In this life the learning was to help others. I would have gotten that from Jason's life as he was helping others, in a way that he would have gotten killed.

L: *Can you tell me about the sleep paralysis that Christine has experienced?*

C: When it happens I experience memories of being in the life selection area, in front of the screen where I chose this life, and watching this life as Christine. It's like a residual of the memory of watching this life before I chose it. It helps to prepare me so I know what's coming and Jordan. I was hesitant to reincarnate this time, I came mostly for Jordan and I still carry the memories very strongly of the other world, it's like I never left. It's involuntary and I didn't understand it.

L: *So now you understand it better, it gives you the power to control it?*

C: Yes.

L: *Can your soul family help you with this, to understand what you can do to switch it on and off when you need it?*

C: Yes, they will help me, otherwise the experiences are frightening.

L: *What is your immortal soul name and the soul names of your soul family?*

C: They call me Miah; my father is called Raylan. My Grandmother is called Murty and Jordan is Sharr. Uncle is called Ashmier. They tell me I'm on track and to keep up the learning. I'm to assist Jordan but not to be pushy and they wish me peace and love.

I asked Christine if there was any other place she would like to visit.

C: Yes, I'm being taken to a big hall, and there are dozens of souls here. They are all lined up on either side, they and clapping. There is 1 Elder who telepathically communicates with me. They are all androgynous, gender doesn't exist. He's wearing the same emblem as my father, a star, but he is not my father. He wants to know why I'm so focused on the gender thing. He is telling me that it was the best choice for longevity. I have to take care of the body, stop treating it badly. I have chosen a body that will last, but I have brought in some issues and weakness from past lives. Being stabbed, hung and crushed and they know I feel it in my body and know I don't understand it. He said I should stay with Jordan and look after her, to try to help her to find her soul family. She doesn't know who they are, and I can help her, I have to be patient with her. They also say I have to be patient with my mother, my mother doesn't want to lose me she has lost me numerous times before in past lives and she tries to control me in this life, she smothers and over protects, a means to control. They are all gathering around me now they feel much bigger than me and are forming a dome of light over me in preparation. I'm like a trainee guide.

L: *Will you have more lives after this life as Christine or is this your last life?*

C: This is the last one, but I will still be a guide but I won't guide through being incarnated it's better without being incarnated because we get more done and people listen to you better.

L: *What do you do when you are back in spirit?*

C: I help my father recreate solar systems, I'm an apprentice. Creating masses of earth and life forms ... I'm no expert, he's the expert.

L: *Do have a sense that there is a higher level of intelligence around you?*

C; Yes, It's just pure joy or love... there is a purity and clarity that you can't describe like pure bliss, a higher level... envelopes everything and all of us.

L: *Are there any entities that can communicate with this higher level?*

C: Yes, the entities that were in the big hall are closer than we are in the soul families, they are much closer.

L: *Can you tell me more about the dome you spoke of earlier, what is this doing?*

C: It feels like it's a healing light that is cleansing me, like a shower of white light. I can see it and feel it coming down over me, it feels wonderful. They are telling me to make sure I survive and keep on this track, this is very important. There is more to learn. I'm trying to find Gail, she's not there. She's part of Jordan's soul family and my brother is in another group completely with my mother. They are not as advanced; they have much more learning to do. This helps me to accept them now.

During a Soul Regression Therapy session, the facilitator speaks directly with the Soul mind of the client as I did with Christine.

When this happens in a place that is perfectly safe for the client, extraordinary things happen. The client will often experience what is called a Jesus moment, an epiphany in which they realize the truth of their soul's karmic journey. They gain an intuitive perception of or insight into the reality or essential meaning of their problem or issue. They begin to understand the true weight or impact of this negative situation or core beliefs and are then able to gain clarity and often they experience a moment of reassessment of their priorities which becomes a major turning point in their life.

After this session Christine felt pleased with what she had learnt about her soul's journey. She decided to make another appointment to come back to see me for weight loss. She was about 10 kilos over weight and pre diabetic, now she understood how she needed to look after her body in her current life and she felt ready to let the excess weight go and start to look after her health. She had been eating food to please her partner Jordan and realised she needed to focus more on her own health.

24. REALISATION THAT DEATH IS NOT THE END

FRED'S PAST LIFE AND BETWEEN LIFE

*Souls are poured from one into another of different
kinds of bodies of the world.*
Jesus Christ in *Gnostic Gospels: Pistis Sophia*

Fred was in his late 60's and recently retired, he travelled quite a long distance to my Brisbane clinic. Fred's wife Jane had died suddenly, she had been chronically ill for most of her life suffering from an autoimmune disease, and lupus. Later in life she had undergone spinal surgery, this had included rods being placed into her spine for support as her bones had become brittle and were collapsing from the illness. Fred had been his wife's carer for many years. She had died in hospital and he was very upset because he wasn't with her when she died, he was having great difficulty letting her go and moving on from her death. He hoped the Soul Regression Therapy sessions would help him to find out if they had lived past lives together and to understand their karmic contract.

He was no stranger to death, his younger brother died tragically in a freak accident at age 3 months, when he rolled off the back seat of a car and broke his neck. Fred was only 2 years old at the time and was the first person to discover the tragedy. He never got over the death of his little brother and felt they had a strong spiritual connection. Further tragedy followed at the age of 3 when his father died. His mother soon remarried and his new step father didn't like him so Fred was sent off to a catholic boarding school at age 4 this left him feeling abandoned by his mother.

Fred was a very good subject for hypnosis and using the Soul Regression Therapy hypnotic induction I guided him back to a past life memory that would help him to understand his connection to his wife and the feelings he experienced of loss and abandonment.

F: It's a shipping port, a lot of bustle and I see sailing ships at the dock, merchant's and people going everywhere it's very busy. I'm a young boy, I have bare feet, and I'm wearing rags, worn trousers and I'm very cold. I'm about 12 years old, I have long brown straggly hair.

L: *How do you feel being there?*

F: Lonely and cold.

I moved him to the place where he lived to find out more about his life.

F: I'm in a lane, a very narrow lane, with buildings each side. I live in one of the rooms off the lane. My room is bare, I have straw to sleep on, I haven't got much. There are 3 other boys here and we share the room. I'm about 15 years old now, but I don't know my true age.

L: *How do you survive?*

F: I do odd jobs, at the docks and run messages.

L: *Tell me about your life, where is your family?*

F: I have always been here, my mother died when I was little and I never knew my father... her friend looked after me after she died, but then she died, she was quite sick and I have no one, no family.

L: *What is your name?*

F: Alan.

L: *Who do you share this room with Alan?*

F: With some other boys, there is Owen, Michael and Herbert, Bert we call him. Owen is the oldest and biggest, he sort of looks after us all because he's the oldest. I think this is England, the docks in London.

L: *How do you feel about your life Alan?*

F: It's not going anywhere; I want to go somewhere, to America, I watch the boats sailing out of the docks and dream of going to a faraway place. I know there are chances for people in America that I don't have here. I dream of stowing away and I'm trying to get a job on a boat, if I can get a job on a boat I will take it. I don't know if I'm strong enough for it though, I'm not very strong.

I moved Alan forward in his life to another event where he was older.

F: I'm in America now, a place called Pittsburgh and it's cold. I'm 30 now and I'm in a city, there are horse drawn carriages and it's snowing, it's so cold. I got a job on a ship in London and we sailed to America. It was a hard job, I ran errands, I cooked and did odd jobs, I was a cabin boy. I'm a labourer now in America, I shovel snow, carry coal, and whatever needs to be done I do it.

L: *Where do you live now Alan?*

F: Not so different to England, I share a room.

L: *How would you describe your life?*

F: It's just as hard as before in England, I'm hungry a lot and cold.

L: *Did anyone help you when you arrived in America?*

F: Yes, there were some Irish people. They took me in, they have family coming all the time from Ireland and they look after outsiders, and they are good people.

L: *Do you live with these people now?*

F: No, that was in New York, I moved away to get work to Pittsburgh. That's where I live now.

L: *How do you feel about moving to America, do you have any regrets?*

F: No, I'm pleased I moved.

I continued moving Alan forward in his life and he arrived at his 51st birthday, he was still living in Pittsburgh.

F: I have a house now, I rent and it's a wood house, it's got 2 stories, it's narrow and in a street where the houses are all along side of one another and it's right up on the street. You walk up the stairs right off the street. I'm still working as a labourer and I have a wife Alice. She's made me a birthday cake. She's a bit younger than me, she has brown hair and she wears one of those long dresses that comes in tight at the waist and comes out. Alice came from Germany and she has a mark on the left side of her face, a scar. She's really nice to me, I think she's Jane. I met her at the market, I was helping one of the stall holders and she was there. We had 2 children, but they both died very young, from Pneumonia.

L: *Does Alice work?*

F: She does charring work, when she can get it.

L: *How would you describe your life now Alan?*

F: It's a hard life, but it's happy, the year is 1836.

I moved Alan further along and he described being in a charity home about age 66. His voice sounded very frail and soft as he continued telling me about his life.

F: I can't work anymore, my strength is gone and I can't support myself, some people took me here. Alice died; she had a chest problem from the cold I think. I had to put her in a pauper's grave, the city did it.

L: *Tell me Alan did you have any interests in your life?*

F: Music, I liked the sound of flute. Sometimes in the tavern I could hear people play the flute and sing. They would sing songs from the old country.

L: *Did you learn to read and write?*

F: I can read a bit and write my name, but not much more. I can read a newspaper slowly.

L: *What is your last name Alan?*

F: Carpenter, but I don't know if that was my born name I think I got that because I did carpentry sometimes.

Alan's life was very simple; he was very poor, but as a young boy he was brave enough to travel from England to America on a ship with the hope of a better life. He had married Alice who he recognised as the soul of his current wife Jane. Alan had made the most of his life even though it was hard, he had remained reasonably happy even though both his children had died very young, he had worked hard as a labourer. Now he was old, weak and alone living in a charity home after his wife Alice had died. I was curious to find out how this life connected to his current life and so I took him to the last day of this life.

F: I'm still in the charity home, I'm in a wooden bed and there is a blanket over me, I don't really feel anything. There are people here not friends, no one I know. I'm glad to go, but I'm cold, always cold, I'm 68 now.

As Alan died he began to describe his death and the journey to the spirit realms often called the Bardo.

L: *What's happening now, how do you feel?*

F: I'm warm; I'm floating away from my body. I see a meadow full of yellow flowers and the sun is shining, it's a beautiful place. I'm alone here, but I don't feel lonely.

I'm comfortable, someone will come. I'm waiting for a guide to come.

L: *Let's just talk some more about that life you lived as Alan. Do you have any regrets from that life?*

F: It wasn't a fun life; it was hard but that didn't matter with Alice there. I regret the children died, I wasn't able to keep them warm. I wish I hadn't broken down I didn't like being in the benevolent asylum. My body wouldn't last, it was never strong, and the work I had to do was too difficult really.

L: *What have you learnt from that life as Alan?*

F: You've got to have a strong body it's important and love, to have someone to love then it's okay. I also learnt the hypocrisy of the religions.

L: *Where did you learn about that?*

F: At the benevolent asylum. They were Protestants there I think, they had no charity in their hearts. They talked of charity, they worked in charity, but they had no charity.

L: *Before you died did you make any decisions about any future lives you might live?*

F: To be strong enough next time physically, to be able to do what I have to do.

L: *Was this life as Alan the life you lived directly before the life you're living as Fred?*

F: Yes it was and I was able to look after Alice in that life as well.

L: *Can you see a pattern between these 2 lives, Alan's life and Fred's?*

F: You have to be strong and be able to look after the people who depend on you. You got to be strong for that. You got to have the money necessary so they aren't cold and they have enough to eat. I see a pattern of not wanting to be hungry and cold and not wanting my family to be hungry and cold. To be able to look after them so they don't die when they are little.

L: *Is this a pattern, if so do you understand this pattern?*

F: Loss is not permanent, it's only temporary. You don't lose them you find them again. My brother this time was too little; I was too little to appreciate that.

Fred was referring to the loss of his little brother who had died at 3 months.

L: *I wonder, was your little brother one of Alan's children who died.*

F: I think he was, he had a very brief stay.

L: *Can you tell me what lessons Fred's family learnt from losing Fred's brother?*

F: He had to teach my mother and my father something. They had to cope with loss.

L: *Yes, and you had to cope with feeling abandon and the loss of your brother.*

F: Yes, a different sort of loss.

L: *And then in the life you lived as Alan you had more loss, your mother died, your children and your wife Alice also died.*

F: That's the nature of being alive isn't it? We love and we lose and we move on and we love again.

I asked him if his soul had lived other lives where he had experienced a similar pattern of loss, abandonment and grief and he said there had been 10 lives.

F: It has been a long slow process to realise that loss is temporary, we meet the people again, and they come again and again. Fred needs to understand this process and to let go of the past.

I continued using the unique Soul Regression Therapy healing process and helped Fred's soul to release the patterns from the past lives of loss, abandonment and grief.

L: *Before we come back is there anyone there who has a message for you?*

He took a long time to answer this question, and when he did his voice was trembling with emotion.

F: Yes, Alice is here and she says she loves me. We have been together for so long, over many lives. We have more lives to live together and more things to do.

Fred realised that he needed to have a strong body to survive it's important and love, to have someone to love then it's okay. I also learnt the hypocrisy of the religions.

L: *Where did you learn about that?*

F: At the benevolent asylum. They were Protestants there I think, they had no charity in their hearts. They talked of charity, they worked in charity, but they had no charity.

L: *Before you died did you make any decisions about any future lives you might live?*

F: To be strong enough next time physically, to be able to do what I have to do. That's the nature of being alive isn't it? We love and we lose and we move on and we love again. It has been a long slow process to realise that loss is temporary, we meet the people again, and they come again and again. Fred needs to understand this process and to let go of the past.

This session brought Fred a lot of peace and created closure around the loss of his wife and also around the loss of his baby brother. He realised that death is not the end and that the soul is immortal and returns many times over and over, and lives different lives with the same soul mates. His wife and brother were both in the past life of Alan.

Because Fred had travelled a long way to see me, he had decided to stay in a local motel for a few days. After this session he decided to come back a few days later to have an advanced Soul Regression session. He realised there were many more questions he wanted answering and a more advanced Soul Regression Therapy session that goes beyond a past life to the afterlife might answer these question for him. He wanted to know who are the members of his soul family and who is his spirit guide, how can he contact this guide. Where should he go to now that his wife had passed, should he leave his home and move to Sydney? The transcript of the session follows.

25. LESSONS OF BETRAYAL AND ABANDONMENT

FRED'S STORY CONTINUED

I should like people to share in my belief in reincarnation.
I think it would cause them to be much happier, much less
frightened, and more sane.
Deneys Keslesy, Psychiatrist & Past Life Regression Therapist.

The opening scene began in darkness, Fred realised he was alone standing in the dark, in some sort of prison. He described wearing a tunic made of rough cloth and said he could hear loud screams and shouts in the background. I regressed Fred further back in time to find out how he came to be in this dark prison cell. As we continue.

F: I'm on a farm, I'm helping my parents, there is a stone house close and I'm 12 years old. We are poor, but the climate is nice, we have enough to eat. I'm in France and my name is Giles. I have 2 sisters, 1 older and 1 younger than me. My father is here, he's called Alfonse, he's broad and has a beard, he's not tall, none of us are tall. I recognise him, he reminds me of my friend George. My mother is nice, her name is Marie and she wears' a dress with her hair tied up. I recognise her; (smiling) she is my mother in my current life. The year is 1397.

L: *Do you go to school Giles?*

F: No, but sometimes the curette teaches me to read. I like to walk in the woods, gather the fruit and look after the animals, I like the animals. I help my father on the property but he has to work for other people too.

I decided to move Giles forward, to the time and circumstances that led him to be imprisoned.

F: There is a war, a holy war and we are being attacked. It's the Bishop and the Kings army, the Catholic army, they say we are heretics. We don't need priests and they have called a crusade against us. I'm 14 years old now, they are rounding us all up and we are being taken away to be burnt. My father was killed, my mother and older sister are being taken by the soldiers, I don't know where my little sister is, she's lost, too much fighting. The village is being burned and the men are being taken away, but because I look young I'm being given a chance to recant, and I'm being taken away to a prison. Now I'm being called before the local inquisitor, he's Dominican. I'm scared, he asks me to repent, to embrace the church and all its teachings or they will kill me like they did my father. My father's dead, they burnt him, I have to make a choice.

L: *Who else is with you on trial?*

F: Yes there are others who will be tried; we all get to have time with the Inquisitor.

L: *What is the inquisitor's name?*

F: I don't know... I have to make a choice he's getting impatient. I chose to recant, I'm too frightened, and I'm not brave enough.

L: *What happens next?*

F: I have to wear a special robe for 2 years, this shows I'm a recanted heretic. I'm to denounce everything I was taught and I can't inherit my father's property. I have to swear an allegiance to the church and I will be burned if I fall or fail any of this. I feel ashamed.

L: *Where do they take you now Giles?*

F: The country side is all ruined it's all burnt; they don't take me anywhere they let me go, they let me find my own way. I go to the orchards and pick up some fruit from the ground. There are others and we are all ashamed about what we have done, but we have no choice really but to survive. None of us want to be burnt alive, some of them are big, there are 12 of us, all boys, my age and older and we live in the woods, we beg and steal to survive.

I took him forward to another event which turned out to be the last day of his life.

F: I'm in a church; I'm 33 years old now. I have been shot by a cross bow and it's very sore, we were raiding, we have become vagabonds. There is a group of us and we raid the properties of the church and the fathers. We steal food, what we can get and I have been shot in the back of the shoulder as I ran away by one of the men of arms. I can't use my left hand and my arm is numb and it's very painful and sore. It's going numb and there is no one to help and I'm dying.

L: *What happens to you?*

F: I'm looking down at my body now, I died.

L: *Do you have any regrets about that life?*

F: I always felt ashamed and I gave in. I wasn't strong like my father was, I was too frightened. I should have been strong enough and gone with him.

L: *You were only just a young boy weren't you?*

F: Yes, I was but I was too scared.

I encouraged him to move beyond to the gateway to the afterlife.

L: *What's happening to you now?*

F: I feel warm and there is a golden soft light and it's a beautiful place and I feel glad to be home. I sense a presence in the light and I feel drawn to it and I'm moving towards it now. There is bright blue light and it's an hourglass shape and it feels like someone has come to meet me. I know this energy is male, it's Alrr.

I explained that he would receive telepathic communication from this guide and to tell me what the guide has to say to him.

F: He says welcome and the energies are merging into mine. It feels wonderful; it takes away the pain, takes away the weakness and makes me feel strong again. Taking away the fear, I feel so much better.

L: *How does Alrr feel about that life you lived as Giles?*

F: He says I have a lot to learn. I tell him I felt ashamed, he says I don't need to but most boys would make the same choice. I tell him I feel bad about being a renegade, but he says in a hard life you have to do what you have to do to survive.

L: *Why did they show you that particular life as Giles, what do they want you to learn?*

F: Sometimes you have to abandon those you love, and sometimes you're going to be abandoned. Sometimes you don't have a choice. I didn't abandon my father, he knew I was too young to take the fire, he didn't mind, he wanted me to survive. In the church where I died I was abandoned, my so called friends left me there, they did what they had to do to survive, I shouldn't judge them they weren't really disloyal just as I wasn't disloyal. But I felt abandoned by them.

L: *They have shown you this life as Giles for you to understand the lessons and experiences your soul is learning about abandonment, the different levels and circumstances so to speak.*

F: Yes it's not always as it seems.

L: *How do you feel about this now?*

F: It will take some absorbing.

L: *What does your guide Alrr say about this?*

F: He's laughing. He says that's why I keep going back to it, I have an issue with loyalty and disloyalty; I have a tendency to be betrayed. But sometimes people have to do what may seem like a betrayal, they are compelled to do what they have to do in their lives, yes.

L: *Does this help you to understand the feelings of loyalty you have felt in the life your living a Fred?*

F: Oh yes, the same issues, I pride loyalty, I admire it and I try and practise it as Fred but I still get betrayed and I have to learn sometimes it's necessary. I have to recognise it will be necessary for people to betray me so that they can grow and I have to learn the lesson (laughing) not to take it so personally. He has a very dry sense of humour.

Fred was communicating with his guide telepathically and interpreting the messages back to me, it would seem his guide had a sense of humour. I went on to ask him to clarify what the lesson was and he said it was more about learning about betrayal than abandonment.

F: Yes I have been abandoned and I feel betrayed, one slips into the other if I'm not careful. I can see this more clearly now it's the leading issue. I have to accept abandonment and not feel betrayed, and understand that it's necessary for people to move on. I should stop feeling sorry for myself (laughing) and to let go, not be so controlling of people in my life. To support them when the current of their life takes them away, to let them go and wish them well. I didn't stop Jane from going, but I didn't do anything to make it easier for her, I could have.

L: *Has the life of Fred gone to plan so far?*

F: Yes it's gone to plan so far, but there were times it could have gone in a different direction, but the outcome would have been the same. Jane would have gone and would have come back; she would have come back for me to look after her.

He was referring here to Jane's soul living the life as Alice in the past life he lived as Alan.

F: We have done this for one another many times, to look after one another. We have to stop grasping and not hold on so tightly at the end. I could have done so much better, if only I knew.

L: *What advice does Alrr have for you about this?*

F: He says to go easy on myself, that I'm slowly getting the hang of it, he stresses slowly that being abandon isn't being left forever, it isn't betrayal either, it's just something they have to do. He says if I search for oneness in everything I can never be abandoned, we are all one in the bigger picture.

L: *Have you been on a search for oneness?*

F: Yes, it's a hunger.

L: *What has prevented your soul from experiencing this oneness, was it because of the feelings of betrayal and abandonment from many lives?*

F: Yes, how can you be one when you're full of resentment,

oneness is a pure place and you can't take that with you, I have to get rid of it, I have to let the resentment go, that's hard.

L: *What does your guide suggest for you to do to let it go, to find peace and oneness?*

F: To stop equating abandonment with betrayal, they are not the same and I have to understand that people have their own lives to live out and they are not there for my benefit only for their development. This is likened to polishing rocks, you put them in a grinder and they grind one another to a polish, that's what we do. Jane and I ground one another to a polish many times.

L: *How do you feel about this now that your beginning to understand this lesson, are you really ready to let this resentment go?*

F: Yes I have got to get past this, and awareness is part of letting it go. I have to stop feeling bad about myself too. He says to stop beating myself up, (laughing) if I was perfect I wouldn't be here.

Fred had experienced an intense and unsatisfied longing for a spiritual experience since he was aged 12, he mediated regularly but he had never been able to connect to his spirit guides. I asked him to ask his guide about this and did this connect in any way to this lesson.

F: Alrr says it's been impossible to get through the static, it's been keeping him out, I didn't realise.

L: *Has your guide been your guide through many lives?*

F: (Laughing) He says how many grains of sand are there on the beach.

L: *Has your guide ever lived with you in a past life?*

F: A long time ago, back in the caves, he was a Sharman, teacher. I was one of his group, clan, I was very raw; he says I'm still a bit raw; he's fun to be around. My friend Terry was in this life, that's why we are so compatible now. He was in the life as Giles; he was one of the group. My sister Janet, she was there, she was a man, and we bump in to one another in different lives.

L: *Is your guide Alrr a guide for them all?*

F: No, not for everyone, but he knows Janet and he's from the rest of us. We are all working on this loyalty issue. Alrr says it's unfinished business for us all and we are all part of the same soul family. We all have our loyalty and betrayal issues, all of us, but not just with one another, with our own families as well. We all work on this issue, some better than others.

L: *Who else is in your soul family?*

F: All my close friends are there, all the people with me. We have come together from all over the world and met up here in Australia, to try our hand at learning our lessons together. Who would think it possible to come from so many countries and to still find each other... but we all did. Alrr says that required a lot of string pulling, (laughing). There are about 12 or 15 souls in my soul family and Jane is there as well, I can see them now.

L: *Would 1 of them like to come forward to speak with you?*

F: They are laughing at me; they say if only 1 comes forward I will feel betrayed by all the others. Jane says she loves me. (His voice began to tremble)

F: She's reminding me of when we were very young, she said she will wait for me forever, and I will never forget it.

L: *Is she waiting for you to return before she reincarnates again?*

F: Yes, we have had many lives together and it's a good possibility there will be many more, and when I get there she will be there. But she will talk to me when she can, she has a lot of recovery to do, she can't project, but she will when she can. I look forward to connecting to her again and I understand why she has to take the time to do what she has to do. She says I always was an impatient devil.

L: *So she will be able to contact you when she restores her energy, but it might take some time because her energy was much depleted from a life of illness.*

F: Yes, that's right.

L: *You have another question, can we ask your guide, why was your life so difficult when you were part of Sidha Yoga?*

F: It revolves around the betrayal and abandonment issues

again, within that organisation the focus of attention is on the Guru, everyone wants to be in the eye of the Guru, but not everyone can be. The person who was the Guru enjoyed the power of that longing that people gave her and played people against each other, it was a power trip. My guide says I can't tell a book by its cover, I have to use the analytical mind sometimes and not be driven by the whole package. He's laughing, he says he thought that after all the lifetimes I have had I wouldn't get involved with religion and I would have been more suspicious. I see it clearly now, it took Jane to walk out on me to be with the Guru, that was the abandonment, and then I walked out on the Guru and I abandoned her. I never even gave it a thought that I might have hurt her by doing that. It's been a steep learning curve, this life as Fred.

L: *Yes but there is still more for you to do as Fred, you're thinking of moving house?*

F: Apparently, Alrr says at my age the outcome is inevitable whatever I chose, (laughing), he's a very plain spoken fella. He says I have to digest what I have been through and that process is just starting and can be done in either place, but I should choose the place that will distract me the least through the process. I have to ask myself if being close to the grandchildren and family will distract me from that. He says what about me, if something happens to me, I have to trust that everything will be taken care of if it becomes necessary. I will be less alone if I moved, but I need to be alone a little bit, but it doesn't really matter because the outcome will be the same. I can't rush this; I have to let it just happen. I have to make the decisions now.

Fred had connected to his spiritual guide, learning his name was Alrr, so I decided to ask Fred what was his spiritual name.

L: *Can you tell me your spiritual soul name?*

F: (pause) Kilar... Kilar.

L: *How do you spell this?*

F: K... i... l... a... r.

L: *What is the meaning of your name?*

F: (laughing) He says, take it easy. He's rather playful.

L: *You have a name that reflects the lessons you're working on.*

F: He says yes that's very appropriate. Kilar, it sounds familiar. He's laughing and says it ought too.

Some of my clients have difficulty remembering or pronouncing their spiritual names. They often say the soul name consists of a vibrational resonance which is difficult to pronounce. The name is felt rather than spoken and the spelling is not as important as the sound. Often they will spell the name rather than pronounce it as Fred did. It's interesting to note that virtually every civilization in the world has had some type of creation myth that involved sound, and that this celestial sound was the first creation, so that everything else created came from such 'otherworldly' sounds. It's no wonder sounds are more important in the spirit world than spelling a name.

L: What is Jane's soul name?

F: Namdoo.

L: *What is the meaning of her name?*

F: Gentle breeze.

L: *If there was a celestial mirror and you were to gaze into the mirror how would you look now, what shape and colour is your energy Kilar?*

F: White, I'm sort of shaped like a capsule, but fluid, moving fluid energy. Blue with some purple in the blue and a little touch of green, the blue and green fluctuate and are shinning. It's a golden sort of a green and the blue is iridescent, I used to see that colour when I meditated. Alrr says of course I did.

L: *Can you tell me Kilar what percentage of your soul's energy did you bring into the body of Fred?*

F: I brought about 60% this time; I knew it would be hard if I needed to be strong.

Research suggests that souls don't bring all their energy into the physical body when they reincarnate, they divide their soul energy often leaving a smaller percentage in the spirit realms, it would seem that the human brain cannot handle 100% energy. The part that remains in the spirit realm still retains the wholeness of the soul and is often called the higher self or over soul. The more experienced the soul is the less energy needed in the physical realms. The soul decides how much energy to bring in and sometimes the soul misjudges which can lead to a difficult and often unhealthy life. When the soul returns home to the afterlife they reunite with their soul energy.

L: *Can your soul connect to this energy, the energy that is always in the spirit world if Fred needs it to be strong?*

F: I don't need that now, but I needed it when I had to look after Jane.

L: *You have a question about your friends Paul and the Guru you followed, Fred wants to know if they are part of his soul family.*

F: Paul is, he's a teacher in the spirit world, and he's very philosophical and wise.

L: *Is he a type of earthly guide for Fred?*

F: Yes you might say that, he doesn't have responsibility for a small group. Alrr says he acts as a ginger, he gingers up people on earth and that's his function. I'm very lucky to have time with him it was a great honour.

L: *What about the Guru, what is the connection with her?*

F: It's some sort of destiny thing. She was learning about how to deal with power and that many, many people made appointments to encounter her. She has a role to play to make people confront their beliefs about spirituality and to rethink what's taught in main stream religions, in her own way she is a ginger group part of a ginger organisation as well, (laughing) but Alrr says she's no Paul. There are power and authority issues that she was working with on a personal level.

I took the opportunity here to ask Kilar what Alrr thought of the regression process that has helped him to connect to his spirit and guide.

F: He says this has very positive benefits and he applauds the work. He says it's very hard the way the world is today to reach people through conventional religion (laughing) you're going through the back door into people's subconscious and that's why Soul Regression Therapy is so effective.

I asked Kilar if his guide wanted to take him anywhere else in the afterlife, most often my clients will visit with a panel or council of Master Guides.

F: He says I will see the council of wise beings soon enough, but they will take me there if I want to go.

L: *Do you want to go?*

F: Yes.

L: *Can you describe your journey there?*

F: We are moving over an urban sort of landscape, gardens, pavements and walks, it's all very beautiful. People are going about their business, souls floating here and there. We are now coming up to a set of stairs, in a marble type of building it's enormous. We are going up the stairs and in through these arched doorways, and now we are in a smaller room. There's a table and looks like there is 4 people there. My guide Alrr is there standing off to the side and I'm standing in front of them.

L: *How do you feel being in front of these Master guides?*

F: They are awesome, but they are very kind, I don't feel in any sense it's a hostile place. It's very supporting.

L: *Those 4 Master Guides, are they male or female?*

F: There is 1 male and 1 female, but the others are more androgynous. They are wearing very bright white robes. The one who looks the most prominent is wearing a very large emerald broach, it's the most brilliant green. One of the others is wearing a silver disc on a chain it has an engraving on it, like a dog running.

L: *What is the meaning of the engraving on the silver disc?*

F: It has to do with loyalty, the dog symbolises loyalty freely given, yes freely given and never retracted. Whatever happens the dog never retracts its loyalty. They say they are pleased with me and they want me to take to heart what I have learnt today. To remember that was the reason I came to earth, and it will help to make this lifetime worthwhile if I remember. Abandonment is not betrayal and resentment should not be held onto, to hold onto love much less tightly and don't try to control everything. He says I have to absorb this and I have been working at this for some time now. I have to absorb it, to take it into the bones.

L: *Is there anything you can do to help you to fully absorb this?*

F: He says I should keep meditating daily, talk to my guide and run it past Allrr.

L: *Is there any special way that will help you to have direct access to your guide Alrr?*

F: He says before I mediate I should tap the end of my

nose with my finger that will help. He says it's good for a mind like mine to meditate daily to be quiet. He also says just remember that I'm loved and to keep on going the way I have been going to the end of the road. I have a tendency to believe I'm not loved and I should never doubt that I am.

L: *How do you feel about all of this now Kilar?*

F: I feel overwhelmed but it's good, positive.

L: *Is there anything else you would like to say to the council before we leave?*

F: I just thank them for their support and I will try to be worthy of their trust. He's smiling and nodded.

At this point I took the opportunity to ask Kilar some questions about his soul journey and the answers were extremely enlightening.

L: *As this meeting comes to a close, can I ask has your soul ever taken an incarnation on any other dimensions or planets other than earth?*

F: Yes, just one other, a gaseous world. It's all pink and orange gas, small swirling gas, there were single molecule creatures drifting through it. We were sort of like tadpoles, tiny microscopic, drifting in the gasses.

L: *Does this world still exist?*

F: Yes it's a long... long way away. This was a very early incarnation, to get used to working ion groups. To be in a group, moving together. Jane was with me in this world, but I don't think any of the others from my group were there, but I'm unsure they may have been there because we moved as a group. When one moved the others all moved.

L: *What do you carry with you today as Fred that you learnt in this world?*

F: To never act alone, when we act it effects the whole of the school, everything is connected.

L: *How does this awareness help you in your current life?*

F: Because you can't be alone, we are never alone. It's just an illusion that we are alone.

Because Fred was in a very deep state of hypnosis and was very receptive to my questions, he was deeply connected to his soul I decided to do some research. I asked Kilar if he is able to connect to a higher dimension or source of energy when his soul is back in spirit and he said he could. I asked him to describe this place to me.

F: Energy, it's just a rippling feeling of energy, there is an undernote or tone of energy that is incredibly harmonious and It changes colour.

L: *Is this a place you frequently visit in spirit?*

F: Yes, and when I'm here I'm not so aware of anything else. There are other souls here, it's a healing place, it's an enormous energy field, it's close to infinity it's huge.

L: *Are these souls networked together or are they*

separate?

F: Both, the unity is experienced through the networking and the suspension of the individuality, but it's suspended not eradicated. It can be taken up again and the individual identity remains so there is no danger that you would ever lose yourself there.

L: *Are they linked directly to a higher consciousness?*

F: It's hard to say, whether the energy itself is the higher consciousness, I suspect the energy itself is the higher consciousness.

L: *Do you feel more in touch with the source in this energy around you?*

F: Yes, it may be a projection from the source itself, it's very close to it. This is a wonderful place; it's more a state of being than a place.

As this session came to an end I asked Kilar what he had learnt from this session and how would these insights impact on his attitude and life in the future.

F: I have to absorb and digest these experiences in this life, in the light of what I have learnt today and in the context of the other lives I'm dealing with the same issue. There is a lot to think about.

Conclusion

An interesting connection existed between the 2 past lives. During the first past life Fred realised he needed to be physically strong to survive the work on the ships, but his body was not strong and it broke down causing an early death. In the second past life he broke down emotionally because he didn't feel strong enough to stand up for his beliefs against religion that had caused his father's death.

Fred realised that sometimes we have to abandon those we love, and sometimes we are going to be abandoned. Sometimes we don't have a choice. He realised he had an issue with loyalty and disloyalty. Fred admired people, who are loyal, and he tried to practise loyalty, but he was beginning to recognise it is sometimes necessary for people to betray him. This was so that they can grow and he could learn the lesson of not taking it so personally, this was his leading issue or lesson.

He understood it was now time to stop feeling sorry for himself and to let go, to not be so controlling of people in his life. To support them when the current of their life takes them away, to let them go and wish them well. He understood his soul contract with Jane was to look after one another and they had lived many lives together and there would probably be more. His guide Alrr told him to go easy on himself, and if he searches for oneness in everything he can never be abandoned, we are all 1 in the bigger picture. He realised that he couldn't have experienced this oneness while he was full of resentment. He also found out that he has up to 15 Souls in his soul family, including Jane and they are all working on similar issues with loyalty, abandonment and betrayal. Not just with one another, but with their own families as well.

His guide wanted him to understand that abandonment is not betrayal and resentment should not be held onto. To never act alone, when we act it affects the whole because everything is connected. We are never alone; we can't be alone. It's just an illusion that we are alone. I contacted Fred 5 years later to see how his life had been affected since he had these sessions with me, below is what he wrote.

You have asked to what extent my life has been affected by the underlying themes revealed in the sessions of abandonment and betrayal since then, and I have to say that those themes have been very much a focus of my life since we did the spiritual regression sessions back in 2010. I continue to process that material and to ponder the degree to which they had an impact on my life, irrespective of whether the regression material was true or more revealing of a metaphorical truth. 2 of my 3 sons have had their partners walk out on them and deny them access to their children, so I have found myself supporting them through experiences that evoked similar emotions. The processing of my own feelings of abandonment has made it easier to assist my sons in the same or similar situations.

I think I have been able to help them release the intensity of their reactions to the situation because of my own processing of those aspects in my life. So to that extent our sessions have been of great benefit and I have found them helpful as mentioned. Fred

How interesting it is that 5 years later Fred's 2 sons had experienced the very same issues with abandonment. Their partners had left them and Fred was now able to help his sons work through the experience because he understood this from a much different perspective. He had integrated the lessons from the sessions. His sons were part of his soul family and the group were all working on the same lessons with their families.

26. A JOURNEY AWAY FROM CANCER

CARLA'S STORY

PART 1

"Your thoughts and beliefs of the past have created this moment, and all the moments up to this moment. What you are now choosing to believe and think and say will create the next moment and the next day and the next month and the next year." Louise L. Hay

Carla was an attractive young woman in her early 30's, she was referred to me by one of my past life regression clients. During the pre-talk I discovered that Carla was married and although she didn't have any children of her own, she had step children. She had never been hypnotised before. When I asked her if she had any health problems I was surprised when she began to tell me she was diagnosed only 12 months ago with incurable lung cancer.

I asked her what treatments she was receiving and she said her condition was incurable and she was not on any medication or treatment plan. I was even more shocked when she told me that 2 other family members also had lung cancer as well. The doctors had told her the condition was genetic. She explained a crazy sequence of events had led to the whole family being screened. Her grandfather and great grandfather on her mother's side had both died from lung cancer. Carla was also experiencing relationship problems with her husband, they had attended a few counselling sessions with no resolve.

She had read books by Brian Weiss and Louise Hays. I asked her if she meditated and she told me she had developed her own strategies to get rid of the cancer and she was feeling pretty comfortable as to where she was at right now. I explained to Carla that I was writing a book about the healing benefits of past life regression and only a few days earlier I had posted a request to my face book page asking for any volunteers who had a serious illnesses and would like to experience a past life regression session so that I could work with them to see if this therapy could benefit them in any way. I asked her what she wanted to find out from the session she was about to have.

She told me she wanted to know if she was connected to her husband, were they connected through past lives they had already lived. Were his children a part of that as well? Because of the cancer being in her lungs, was she holding onto something in her lungs? Part of the reason for the session was to find out who she was in a past life and another part wanted to know anything that would help with her condition. I asked her to tell me more about her relationship with her husband. She explained she wanted more from him, for him to help her more, especially with the kids. She felt he had shut down and wasn't coping with her illness. Carla wanted him to support her on an emotional level. He was just carrying on with everyday life as though everything was normal. She wanted him to be more interested and understanding about the alternative therapies she was researching and experiencing. Her juicing and organic foods were important for her healing and he seemed disinterested in this. She thought he was avoiding taking about her illness so that he didn't have to accept she had cancer.

Before her diagnosis he had been overly attentive to her needs, especially if she was sick, now he was just the opposite. As she looked back on their life together since they married she realised she wanted more from him now. She said he was in a place where he thought that it didn't matter what he did, nothing would ever be good enough for Carla. She felt it was easier being the person with cancer, rather than being the person to support the person with cancer.

I began to share a little about my personal experience when my late partner Brian was dying from Melanoma cancer. Brian was only 50yrs old when we found out he had cancer; he was in complete denial that he might die and wanted to fight it all the way. He thought he would find a cure, even at the end he still didn't accept he wasn't going to make it. I had to explain to him that the chances of a recovery were very small, his body was already too far gone, the cancer had consumed most of his organs. He needed to tell his daughter where he was at, and ask her to come over because the chances were he wasn't going to be alive longer than a week. He took the attitude that if he didn't acknowledge he had cancer it wouldn't happen. He had shut down emotionally and wouldn't talk about how he felt. It was a very difficult time in my life, I took time off work and was there for him every step of the way, supporting him, taking him to hospital appointments for treatments and radiation therapy. He was super independent and wanted to do everything on his own. I explained my experience to Carla with the hope she would understand that everyone handles cancer differently, the patient and the family. She thought it was easier for her to be the one who has the cancer, but in my experience it was just as difficult trying to help my partner who was in denial of his condition. I explained that both my late partner and her husband experienced what Elizabeth Kübler-Ross described as the extended grief cycle.

On the web site: http://changingminds.org/disciplines/change_ management/kubler_ross/kubler_ross.htm they explain this cycle and how Kübler-Ross came to discover it. Below is an extract from this web site.

Elizabeth Kübler-Ross was a doctor in Switzerland who was very unhappy about the way doctors treated the terminally ill.

She spent a lot of time with dying people, both comforting and studying them. She wrote a book, called 'On Death and Dying' which included a cycle of emotional states that is often referred to (but not exclusively called) the Grief Cycle. She discovered that this emotional cycle was not exclusive just to the terminally ill, but also to their families and other people who were affected by bad news, such as losing their jobs or otherwise being negatively affected by change. The important factor is not that the change is good or bad, but that they perceive it as a significantly negative event.

The Extended Grief Cycle

The Extended Grief Cycle can be shown as in the chart below, indicating the roller-coaster ride of activity and passivity as the person wriggles and turns in their desperate efforts to avoid the change.

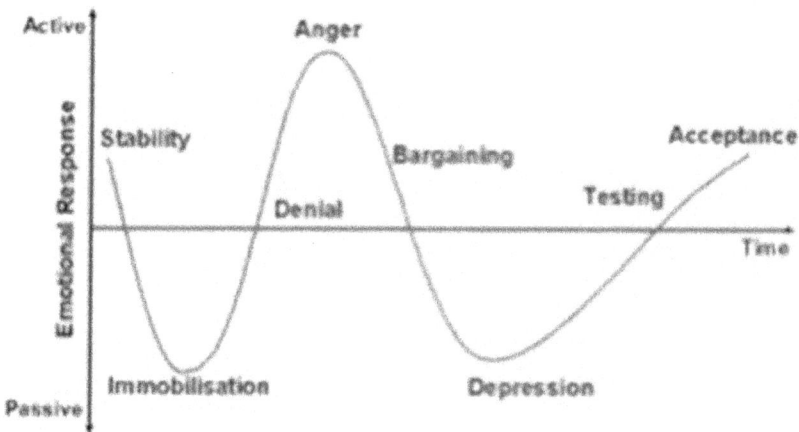

The initial state before the cycle is received is stable, at least in terms of the subsequent reaction on hearing the bad news. Compared with the ups and downs to come, even if there is some variation, this is indeed a stable state.

And then, into the calm of this relative paradise, a bombshell bursts...

- Shock stage*: Initial paralysis at hearing the bad news.
- Denial stage: Trying to avoid the inevitable.
- Anger stage: Frustrated outpouring of bottled-up emotion.
- Bargaining stage: Seeking in vain for a way out.
- Depression stage: Final realization of the inevitable.
- Testing stage*: Seeking realistic solutions.
- Acceptance stage: Finally finding the way forward.

A common problem with the above cycle is that people get stuck in one phase. Thus a person may become stuck in denial, never moving on from the position of not accepting the inevitable future. When it happens, they still keep on denying it, such as the person who has lost their job still going into the city only to sit on a park bench all day.

Getting stuck in denial is common in 'cool' cultures where expressing anger is not acceptable. The person may feel that anger, but may then repress it, bottling it up inside. Likewise, a person may be stuck in permanent anger (which is itself a form of flight from reality) or repeated bargaining. It is more difficult to get stuck in active states than in passivity, and getting stuck in depression is perhaps a more common ailment.

Another trap is that when a person moves on to the next phase, they have not completed an earlier phase and so move backwards in cyclic loops that repeat previous emotion and actions. Thus, for example, a person that finds bargaining not to be working may go back into anger or denial. Cycling is itself a form of avoidance of the inevitable and going backwards in time may seem to be a way of extending the time before the perceived bad thing happens.

In the past Carla had felt really close to her husband, they had been together for quite a few years, marrying only weeks before she found out about her cancer. He was extremely devastated and very angry with the diagnosis. The anger was probably because their future together was now uncertain and his dream of having a happy family life together would be shattered if she died. It was no wonder he became withdrawn and almost in denial of her condition. He was experiencing the first 3 stages of the grief cycle.

Carla on the other hand was trying to be very positive; she was focusing on healing herself, by reading positive books, keeping her mind positive and changing her diet to juices and organic food. She had not had any surgery, chemotherapy or radiation treatment for the cancer because they told her the condition was incurable, but not having any treatment was actually in her favour.

In the book "Clean Up your Act" written by Ramiah J Selwood he discusses his theory about such treatments. "Doctors may tell you chemotherapy and radiation has a good chance of working, because that's what they have been told at medical college by the suppliers of the chemicals - Big Pharma. But as with me and my family, if you do your research you will find that chemotherapy treatments may only improve your chances of living beyond 5 years by 2 percent."

Carla strongly believed she would survive the cancer. She was on a positive wellness cycle where she was not only detoxing her body by changing her diet, she was also detoxing her mind by reading positive books, meditating and looking into her past lives to clear and heal the past.

She had stopped going for scans because the radiation could give her breast cancer or leukaemia. She said she didn't think about her condition unless she received a letter about an appointment for a scan. Basically she was just trying to lead a normal life, getting plenty of exercise and she was still working. She felt tired most of the time but she listened to her body feedback and went to bed early and rested when she needed to. I explained that we would attempt to connect her to a past life memory that might help her to understand her current life better, the health challenges she was experiencing and any karmic contracts she might have made. If her husband was in the past life, then we might be able to find out more about their connection. Carla was a very good subject for hypnosis, relaxing quickly she slipped into a deep hypnotic state.

The session follows.

L: *Where are you now... look around.*

C: It feels like I'm not anywhere.

L: *Is it light or dark around you?*

C: Dark.

L: *Are you inside or outside?*

C: Outside.

L: *Describing your surroundings... where do you find yourself?*

C: It's a market.

L: *Can you describe how it looks.*

C: Wooden carts... fruit and vegies in them.

L: *Is this a warm day or is it cold?*

C: Warm... sunny.

L: *Do you see people?*

C: Yes, the marketplace is busy.

L: *Can you describe the people that you see, how do they look, what are they wearing?*

C: They feel taller.

L: *Tall, taller than you?*

C: Yes

L: *Are up a male or female?*

C: I'm a girl.

L: *How old are you little girl.*

C: I feel 9.

L: *Are you with anyone at the market?*

C: No.

L: *Do you wear anything on your feet?*

C: No.

L: *What about your clothing... how does that look?*

C: It feels old, rags.

L: *What about your hair, how's that?*

C: Dirty.

L: *As you're standing there in the market, how are you feeling?*

C: Hungry.

L: *What are you thinking about?*

C: How I'd get some food.

L: *So what are you going to do, is there any food... or something you can get?*

C: I feel hopeless.

L: *So where is your family, do you have anybody?*

C: I don't feel like I do.

L: *Does anybody notice you?*

C: No.

At this point I move Carla slightly forward in this lifetime as we continue

L: *Let's move forward a little way.*

C: I live in like a shack with a bed, by myself.

L: *How did you find this place?*

C: It feels like I just knew.

L: *Knew where to go? Are there any other people around you at all? Just get a sense of this place where you are. Is it a city?*

C: It's country. Like an old town.

L: *Do you remember what happened to you? What happened to you to be in this place alone?*

C: No. It just feels like it's always been like this.

I move Carla further forward again to a turning point in that lifetime. As we continue

L: *Where are you now?*

C: In a cleaner house. I've met a man.

L: *How old are you now?*

C: In my 30's.

L: *And your life's better with this man?*

C: Yes

L: *Are you married?*

C: No... we're just together.

L: *So tell me how do you look now that you're older?*

C: Pretty.

L: *What type of house do you live in? Is it a wooden house or a brick house?*

C: I see shiny floors. A brick house.

L: *looking back on your life... what happened to you, how*

did you get from there to where you are now?

C: Kept trying.

L: *Did someone take you in?*

C: Yes, I think my partner did but not in a bad way.

L: *Is he older than you?*

C: Yes, I would say 40's but you know it was a friendship at the start.

L: *So he helped you? How old were you when you met him?*

C: 27.

L: *And you lived on the street all those years?*

C: And in my shack.

L: *And how did you survive?*

C: I stole food. I washed in a lake.

L: *Are you still in the same place where the shack was?*

C: Somewhere else.

L: *And did you move there with him?*

C: Yes.

L: *What is the name of this place?*

C: Norman.

L: *Norman?*

C: Yes... it starts with 'N'

L: *What country would this be?*

C: England.

L: *Do you have a sense or a feeling of what year, What time period this is?*

C: I feel like it's early 1900s.

L: *And your partner, this man that you're with... what do you call him, He's very special to you isn't he, what is his name?*

C: I don't know his name.

L: *So how does he look; can you describe him?*

C: He's got brown hair... tall and strong. But very soft.

L: *Do you recognise this man?*

C: No.

I had thought this man may have been Carla's husband, but she didn't recognise him.

L: *And what does he do? What type of work does he do to support you?*

C: Office... something...

L: *And you work?*

C: No.

L: *Do you have children?*

C: No... I'm happy in the garden.

L: *Do you remember how you got to be on the streets?*

C: No.

L: *You were just a young girl. What happened to your family? Do you remember having a family?*

C: No.

We move forward once again in that past lifetime to another turning point as we continue.

L: *Where are you now?*

C: I feel like I'm old and my husband's old. We're retired. We're happy sitting on the porch.

L: *Are you still at the same house?*

C: No.

L: *You've moved?*

C: To a cottage with a porch.

L: *And did you have any children?*

C: No.

L: *And what does your husband call you, what is your name?*

C: Margie

L: *Can I call you Margie?*

C: Yes

L: *And what do you call your husband?*

C: John

L: *And how do you feel about John?*

C: I love him

L: *How would you describe your life together?*

C: Peaceful.

L: *Do you have any particular interests in your life, things that you like to do?*

C: Reading... gardening.

L: *And did you ever travel?*

C: No, we were happy.

I moved her forward to the last day in this life, to Margie's death, where she found herself sick in her bed.

L: *Do you know what sickness you have?*

C: A cold or pneumonia... nothing terrible... but I'm just tired.

L: *And where is John... is he there with you?*

C: Yes.

L: *And have you been sick for long?*

C: No

L: *What else are you aware of?*

C: I'm in a dressing gown, like a nightie, with the blanket on me, and my hair's grey and in a bun. I feel like there's a doctor there... but it's too late.

L: *Do you know that it's too late?*

C: Yes, I'm floating.

L: *How does it feel?*

C: It feels like I'm just a ball of light looking over the room from the corner.

L: *What's happening down there in that room?*

C: I feel like I've let John down.

L: *Why do you feel that way?*

C: Because I was tired... (crying)

L: *What thoughts and feelings do you have as your soul leaves that body?*

C: There's nice people out there.

L: *There's nice people out there... because he looked after you didn't he... how old were you?*

C: 82

L: *Was it a shock that you died?*

C: I knew... John didn't know.

L: *He didn't know, ah, it was a shock to him, what's your concern now?*

C: (crying).

L: *Are you worried about him?*

C: I should have told him.

L: *What should you have told him?*

C: That I knew that I was going... instead of not saying anything... because I thought that was better than saying something... stupid.

L: *You thought you should have prepared him.*

C: Yes, because he would've listened.

L: *How does that life connect to your current life?*

C: I need to talk... I need to stop... I need to show my true feelings instead of pretending I'm strong and saying nothing... thinking it's better than saying something... so then he understands... because he will understand.

L: *So as Carla you've been keeping your feelings to yourself and pretending to be strong?*

C: Yes, because I had to when I was by myself.

L: *When you were single?*

C: When I was a girl in the market place.

L: *That was a hard childhood growing up.*

C: I did ask for help.

L: *But you were smart... you learnt to rely on yourself.*

C: I knew I could do it myself... and I'd rather do that than ask for help.

L: *And is that something that Carla does... tries to be strong?*

C: Yes.

L: *And has she needed to be strong, growing up in her life as well?*

C: Yes.

L: *In what way?*

C: For my family.

L: *To be the strong one in the family.*

C: I do feel I am.

L: *So what's happening now, Is it light or dark around you?*

C: Light.

L: *Do you feel you're moving?*

C: No... just standing.

I decided to ask Carla's higher mind to help her to understand the lessons from the past life and the connections to her current life as Carla.

L: *Carla has some questions... you've shown her that life Margie... what more does she need to know about this connection?*

C: It's ok to be tired. You don't have to be strong. You don't have to hide that you're tired.

L: *So she needs to speak up more to her husband so he'll understand how she's really feeling.*

C: Yes.

L: *Can you give her some information about this condition, that's causing her to feel so tired?*

C: She just needs more energy. It's the mind.

L: *So tell me more about the mind... what is this?*

C: Clear the mind, you'll have more energy.

L: *What is it in her mind that she needs to clear it... what's going on in there?*

C: Thinking about everything.

L: *She worries or just processes?*

C: Processes and organises so that everyone else is happy. But it doesn't matter.

L: *It doesn't make things, just wears her out.*

C: Yes.

L: *Takes her energy and she needs this energy now to heal her body, is that right?*

C: Yes.

L: *So can you help her now to let go of this overly processed mind... to clear the mind... to let go of all those busy thoughts that don't help. Is that something that we could do now?*

C: That would be good.

L: *So how could you do that; can you do a scan in her mind?*

C: Put it all in the bin.

L: *Put it all in the bin, that busy, busy stuff, planning and organising and always putting everyone before yourself, is that what you've been doing?*

C: Yes, it's annoying.

L: *It's annoying, just letting it all go, those silly, busy thoughts, taking all that energy, stopping you sleeping properly at night.*

I help her to clear all of this using a skillset of techniques gained from many years of experience as a past life therapist

L: *Is it cleared for now?*

C: Yes.

L: *How does that feel?*

C: Open.

L: *Let me ask, is there anything that she needs to know?*

C: It's ok to have a nap, you don't have to be awake all the time.

L: *It's ok for you to rest when you're tired?*

C: It doesn't matter.

L: *Is there anything else, any diet changes, anything Carla can do to help herself, to speed up her recovery?*

C: In the mind.

L: *Carla has chosen this particular body, as a soul, to come into this body, into this family, to be with these other souls... what is it that Carla is learning from her family by experiencing these issues with the body?*

C: Different people get it and it doesn't matter how old you are... 3 people deal with it in 3 different ways.

L: *It's not a good thing that people deal with it differently, is there one better way?*

C: You have to deal with it.

L: *And some don't deal with it.*

L: *What is it that you can do to help your family, is there anything, or is this a lesson to learn?*

C: I don't think so.

L: *So looking back on the life you lived in the market place, look at the situation that you are in now, you could have easily given up, but you didn't give up did you, your soul doesn't give up easy does it?*

C: No.

L: *Knowing that now, what is the main theme of your soul, is it to always push forward?*

C: Yes, just throw anything at me and I'll deal with it.

L: *But you've had help, you had help from John and you accepted his help, so it's to know when to be strong and when to seek help?*

C: Yes.

L: *This connection to your family, are they to learn from you about this... maybe you're here to set an example for them?*

C: Show them what to do.

L: *Show them how to manage.*

C: You can still do everything... you don't have to stop everything.

L: *And sometimes you know that showing is better than words, just doing?*

C: Yes.

L: *Sometimes we can't save other people either, it's their journey to learn or not to learn.*

C: Yes.

L: *With your journey, as you move forward, as you become more strong, I'm wondering if you get a sense or a feeling of the purpose of this now... the purpose of your journey in your current life and how it connects with the other life?*

C: I need to talk more.

L: *Speak up more about how you feel?*

C: Yes, to everyone... just show them that there's a way.

L: *To be a spokesperson... not to bury it, to speak up, let them know.*

C: (crying)

L: *That's right, and not to give up, not to allow those doctors to put you down or make you feel like they're in control.*

C: I can't give up; I need to talk now.

L: *So is that something you feel you can do now?*

C: I feel like I can do it... I'm strong... but I don't feel like... I don't know... I don't feel like people will listen... I'm scared they won't listen. And I don't want to look like I'm just looking to be a victim... or for attention... so I'm scared.

L: *Scared of what they'll think, that they'll judge you?*

C: That they'll think I'm doing it for attention... for poor me... but it's not.

L: *I guess it's how you say it really, if you could find a way.*

C: Because you have to find the balance of not being a victim but not shoving it in people's faces.

L: *It's finding that balance. Maybe you could write your story and share it, that's one way. Now you understand this perhaps you'll have more insight as to what you can do to balance that out?*

C: Yes, I don't pick the right words... that's kind of the problem... I think I'm saying it right... to me it sounds right... but he's like my audience... I have to be mindful of my audience.

L: *That's right... it's not what you say it's how you say it. That's something perhaps you can learn?*

C: I need to learn that.

L: *How to communicate feelings in a positive light without coming across as a victim?*

C: I don't feel I am communicating it because it's not being received in the way that I intended it to be received. I don't want to fight, ever, I just want it to be peaceful.

L: *Well this may take you some time to learn, to practice. Maybe go and get some help with this in some way. There is a way, you'll find... it will come to you... but being aware of it is the first step, isn't it... to move towards that. You've shone the light on this now... you're seeing it differently, through different eyes. So how does that feel seeing it differently?*

C: Light. I feel like it's easy.

L: *So you just have to be yourself... speak from your heart?*

C: Not think so much.

L: *Not thinking... not use your head so much.*

C: Don't analyse everything... just say it.

L: *It's about letting go of all of those thoughts and just going with how you feel.*

C: Yes, the first feeling, not pushing them down.

L: *This path that you're moving in a new direction with your work and your study... how do you feel now, about this?*

C: Excited.

L: *You're on the right path then aren't you?*

C: I just want to be there.

L: *So it's all going to come into play - all these little parts... learning about your intuition and perhaps speaking in a better way... connecting to the training... Doreen Virtue's workshop... connect to your inner self.*

C: Be in the moment

L: *Be in the moment, what about the future, do you think that children are something that you could be looking at?*

C: Yes.

L: *Once you get this sorted out and get back on track.*

C: Yes, at 35.

L: *35?*

C: But something will happen at 33, but 35 is fine. I've got lots to do between now and then.

L: *How do you feel about this now that you've had all these insights and this information?*

C: I just feel normal, like it's not as bad as I thought it was... it's fine.

L: *It's learning. You can't know what you don't know until you learn it. you're understanding it deeper now... because that woman that you were, Margie, she's going to be just fine... maybe, she wants you to do what she couldn't do... to speak up... now John could be there now, and they're reunited... and if you could see him there now, what would you say to him?*

C: Sorry, it's ok to have sorrow.

L: *You know he probably knew. If he could speak to you now, what would he say?*

C: It's ok.

L: *Does his energy feel familiar?*

C: I don't know... it feels as though he's separate.

L: *Part of a different life?*

C: Yes.

L: *Maybe part of your soul family. We have many soul friends that we reincarnate with over periods of time, from different lives.*

C: Maybe grand-dad. because I don't know my grand-dad, but I feel it's him. His eyes.

L: *So they're going to be fine now, John and Margie... they're going to go... they need to go... because they are together... and you're now connected to the energy of Carla who you are now in your current life.*

At this point I do some more healing with Carla. She releases further residue that no longer serves her, leaving it all behind in the past so she can lead a more positive balanced current life. As we continue.

L: *What's going to be different... to make sure you have a more positive more balanced life?*

C: Rest... not feeling guilty for resting... because I think about that. I feel like I'm being judged, but no-one is... if you sleep.

L: *That's right. You can take the time to rest more... it's ok.*

C: Totally ok.

L: *Good, you're doing really well.*

The life of Margie and John was very happy. John rescued her from a lonely life and at the end as Margie died she felt she had let John down because she knew she was going to die but didn't tell him. She realised he would have listened to her had she told him. She also realised that she needed to talk more to John, she should have showed him her true feelings instead of pretending she was strong, he would have understood. She realised there were connections between the life as Margie and her current life as Carla, because as Carla she had a pattern of keeping her true feelings to herself as well. She had pretended to be strong when she found out she had cancer. Her soul had learnt to survive by being independent and strong and internalizing her feelings so she could survive the difficult childhood as Margie.

Carla realised that this was a pattern through her life because she felt she had to be strong when her mother was diagnosed with cancer, she took on the role as the strong one in her family. She realised she didn't always have to be the strong one in the family and she needed to stop hiding her feelings about being tired, she needed to let her family know when she was tired.

I took the opportunity here to ask some questions about her condition and why she was so tired. Carla's Higher Mind told me that it was her logic mind that was causing the tiredness. Her logical mind over processes, worries and organises to keep everyone else is happy. Because her mind is always worrying this is what was taking her energy and causing her to feel tired all the time. She needs this energy now to heal her body, so I asked her Higher Mind to do a healing and help her to let go of all this overly processing and worrying. Once this was done Carla immediately felt more open.

I decided to see if I could find out what the soul reasons were for the cancer, not just her own illness but the connections between other family members as well. It was important not to be a victim and not to give up. By Carla being the strong one in the family she could show her family how to keep fighting. Carla realised she needed to speak up to do this, but part of her was still scared people wouldn't listen. And she didn't want to look like she was a victim. It was about finding the balance of not being a victim, but not shoving it in people's faces. To speak up in the right way, speak from the heart, being in the moment.

27. LESSONS OF ACCEPTANCE AND FORGIVENESS

A JOURNEY AWAY FROM CANCER

CARLA'S STORY CONTINUES

*Forgive the past. It is over. Learn from it and let go.
People are constantly changing and growing. Do
not cling to a limited, disconnected, negative image
of a person in the past. See that person now. Your
relationship is always alive and changing."*
Dr Brian Weiss

Carla came back for a second session about a year later and I was very surprised to hear how the first session had helped her to change her life. Carla told me that the session had helped her to understand an important soul lesson about communication. She went home after the first session with me feeling confident that she could now communicate her needs to her husband in a more open way. She decided to start over with a completely new attitude. Carla practised this more open approach of communication for a few months, but their relationship didn't improve it took a downhill turn when he stopped talking to her and shut down even though Carla had made a conscious effort to bring her family together.

The first session we had done had opened her up to think seriously about her life and future, she especially kept in mind the premonitions that something very significant might happen when she turned 33 and possibly she would have a child when she was 35. Eventually Carla made the difficult decision to leave her husband.

Since the session Carla had attended a Doreen Virtue workshop which had helped her to connect more deeply to her inner guidance and her angels. Even though she knew she had to leave, she struggled to do this, sitting with the idea for a while, but eventually she felt strongly guided to leave. So she packed a bag and left, as she drove away she felt emotionally distraught, Carla couldn't focus on her driving because of her emotional state, so she stopped the car to compose herself and as she looked up she noticed a sign with the numbers 444. In Doreen Virtues book "Angel Numbers 101", she states that one of the most common ways in which angels speak to us is by showing us repetitive number sequences and the numbers 444 means thousands of angels surround you at this moment, loving and supporting you. You have a very strong and clear connection with the angelic realm, and are an Earth angel yourself. You have nothing to fear—all is well.

This synchronistic message came at just the right moment for Carla and helped her to realise she had made the right decision in leaving her husband and gave her the courage to move beyond the fear and focus on her future. A week later she resigned from the long standing job she had been working in for many years and she moved to the Gold Coast. She took a plunge into living a life that was more authentic to whom she was becoming and she also felt more freely able to communicate to the people around her. At this point Carla remembered the past life as Margie and how she had overcome many difficulties. This helped her to remain strong and focused. Her scans showed the lung cancer was still there, but now she was using alternative therapies to heal and she had met a natural health practitioner who was very knowledgeable in alternative methods to heal cancer. Carla was now celebrating 2 years since she was first diagnosed. Her first diagnosis was stage 4 which the medical profession say is incurable. Medically they only give people with this level of cancer 5 years to live with treatment and surgery. Without medical treatment they don't expect the person to survive very long at all.

Carla said she felt the cancer had come into her life to lead her to a different place, and she believed the cancer would go when she was at the place she needs to be. The doctors believed the cancer was genetic coming down through her mother's side of the family. Carla wanted to go back to look at a past life that might help her further on her soul's journey and to understand what she was meant to learn from the cancer.

As the first scene opened up, she described herself as wearing very prestigious clothing fit for a Queen. She was a young female with long sun kissed hair standing in a village with her father who it seemed was the King. I asked her to describe this life and she said it was a happy, peaceful, abundant life. Her name was Giselle and she laughed when she told me how easy this life was. I asked her to tell me more about this easy life and she said she had a brother but her mother had died when she was 6. I decided to move her forward find out more about her life as Giselle. She had taken over from her father who was very sick and much older now. Giselle was 43 and married to a lovely man, they had 2 children. Her role was to make decisions for the village and her husband Richard helped her with this duty. The location was in Greece and the village was called Athene. We pick up the dialogue as I move her forward in this past lifetime.

C: I'm at home... my son has grown... to take over from me now... I'm old... I'm 83... I'm tired.

L: *Is your husband still there, Richard?*

C: Yes.

L: *And your father, he's passed now?*

C: Yes, that was ok.

L: *What do you call your son?*

C: Amal.

L: *And how do you feel about him?*

C: He's great, a good person. He's happy.

L: *And the villagers, how do they feel Amal taking over from you?*

C: No one likes change, but they're happy... they know he'll do a good job

I guided Giselle to the last day of her life.

C: I'm at home in bed, my whole family's around me... my husband's there, my daughter, my son...

L: *How old are you now?*

C: 92.

L: *Are you just old or do you have something wrong with you?*

C: Just old.

L: *And how do you feel about your death?*

C: Peaceful... we just know that it's not the end.

L: *You have beliefs in the afterlife?*

C: Yes... they'll be able to look after me... I'm going to another place now.

L: *How do you feel about your death?*

C: Fine... excited about what lies ahead.

L: *What about those below, still around your bed, your family. Are you able to communicate to them at all, now that you've left that body?*

C: They know it's ok... they can feel their hearts warm up when I communicate with them.

L: *So what happens now, Is it light or dark around you?*

C: Light.

L: *Do you feel that you're moving?*

C: I'm just there... anywhere I want to be... time is irrelevant. I don't have a body, I just am... me.

L: *As you look back on that life, it was such an idyllic life.*

C: It's possible... it's possible for everyone.

I asked her why she had been shown that particular life and how did it connect to the life she was living as Carla.

C: It's all about love. It's the place you have to come from.

L: *It's all about love. The family that you lived with... but even though that life was very easy and simple, was there anything going on beyond where you lived, was there any wars of disruptions.*

C: Yes, but it was easy for us to live in that place of love because we didn't go beyond the walls... you have to... you have to spread the love.

L: *It was safe there... you didn't go beyond... you didn't want to.*

C: It was the easy option.

L: *So why do you think you've been shown that life, how does it connect to your life now? Which is a very different life.*

C: To spread the love, to go beyond the walls and show people that it's possible... love can heal everything.

L: *So to spread the love you need to go beyond the walls... to help those people that are out there further?*

C: (crying).

L: *So what's the deep truth behind this connection to your current life, why do you think you need to experience this life as Carla?*

C: Because the life where it was easy... so easy... before... but this one... I can show people you can make it easy... you can love even through the worst things... just have to find yourself again.

Carla was beginning to understand the connections between the 2 lives, Giselle's easy life and the difficult life she was the one she was presently living as Carla. Giselle's life was only easy because she lived within the safety of the village walls, she was protected from the war and pain in the outside world. She had taken an easy safe option. Carla's lesson was to venture beyond what was comfortable and known, to go beyond the confinement and protection of the marriage. To show people that it is possible to heal and love at the same time and that love can heal everything. That you can love even through the worst things, but it is important to be true to yourself. Carla was now on this journey. I connected Carla to her higher soul mind and began asking more questions to help to clarify the insights.

L: *Why have you shown her that particular life, that perfect life?*

C: I need to learn as much as I can... don't stay within the walls.

L: *So can you help Carla to understand more about this?*

C: She has to work with the light. It's coming.

L: *It's coming, Is that a healing light?*

C: Healing and all knowing.

L: *Ok, so can you go ahead and explain more about this, because she really wants to know about her future.*

C: The pain in her heart will go.

L: *Tell me about this heart pain that she's carrying.*

C: Unforgiveness.

L: *So who doesn't she forgive?*

C: Some family members... she's working so hard to forgive... she will get there... this was to show her that you don't have to sit in that place and be a victim... just work with the light and shine through... be a shining light.

L: *What is your true soul purpose, what are you here on earth to do, this time.*

C: To help people discover who they are.

L: *Just like you're doing... and I guess you can't really help unless you've walked in those shoes can you... felt the life, the emotion, the pain... to know that it can be healed, that you can forgive.*

C: I can forgive.

L: *That's right... you can forgive yourself for not forgiving yourself sooner.*

C: Yes

L: *What is it that you're to speak about... to help these people... what's your message?*

C: I see the words happiness and love.

L: *The message is to be happy and to love?*

C: They're the words that come through. To speak about it.

L: *To speak about it... because the life that you lived as Giselle was very happy... it was full of love and joy.*

C: It's just a thought and you can change your thoughts... so to be unhappy to happy is just a matter of looking at it differently. You don't have to stay there... you don't have to do anything that you don't want to do... you don't have to be who society or your family around you want you to be... just don't even worry about it. There's still another message... it's going to come... it'll come.

L: *Can you help Carla to understand this connection with the cancer, and with her family members with cancer*

C: It's god's plan. it's just part of god's creation.

L: *She made a decision... she wanted to take that disease away from her family.*

C: She was going to get it anyway.

L: *Why's that?*

C: It was like a launch pad to push her forward... she was stagnant where she was... she wasn't living to her true potential.

L: *But she is now, isn't she?*

C: She's on the right path... she's the healer.

L: *Help her to understand, what does she need to do to heal.*

C: Go ahead with her plans. It's the stomach. It holds a lot of stuff there.

L: *Emotion.*

C: Yes, she needs to release that. The lungs have captured the bad things that are going on in the body, to encapsulate it so that it doesn't go through the blood or anywhere else... all these sick feelings, relationships, thoughts, food, everything... they've just been captured there and the lungs are holding them safely.

L: *The lungs are holding them safely and do they need to continue to do that?*

C: Until the time's right.

L: *And when will the time be right?*

C: Soon... she's not going to get sick from it... not sick... sick on paper yes, but not physically sick... it'll go before that happens. She just had to.

L: *So this is a build up from all her life, from the stuff that happened growing up, from the parents, and with her husband.*

C: But also so she knows... she knew what it was like to be told those things... and then to live it.

L: *So she took it on physically.*

C: And once she's learnt everything that she's supposed to, it'll go.

L: *It'll dissolve.*

C: As quick as it came.

L: *Oh, good.*

L: *To finalise it all. To cut the cords and the ties.*

C: Yes, stop holding back and being afraid to send that final.

L: *She needs to get on and do it, and that will release.*

L: *So let me just ask you this question, have you always just had lives on earth, or have you ever lived somewhere else, on other planets or other realms.*

C: An angel.

L: *You were an angel?*

C: Helping people.

L: *Where were you when you did this?*

C: Everywhere.

L: *So what made you choose... why did you choose to come into an earth body and have a life?*

C: I can help more people.

L: *And did you have others that encouraged you to have physical lives... did they ask you to do this?*

C: God did.

L: *So who is this God that you describe... how would you describe that energy?*

C: The light that we all come from.

L: *And are there others with a higher level than you, that you communicate with... that are connected to that higher light?*

C: Yes, the ones that have been... many, many... for eternity... yes.

L: *When you're back home in the spirit form... what happens to you... what do you do when you're there?*

C: We have meetings about Earth... and how we can help heal it because otherwise it's going to implode on itself.

L: *You have meetings on how to best help. That's one of the reasons you've come... to help... to prevent that from happening. And how do you feel, do you feel that this is going to help?*

C: Yes... feel empowered.

L: *There's a lot of you helping now isn't there?*

C: Yes.

L: *And do you have a particular guide that helps you... that you are able to communicate with... a spiritual Master guide?*

C: The archangel Michael... and God.

L: *Asking this higher knowledge and wisdom, what's the best course for Carla... what's the best way for her to help people to heal... she's done nutritional study, and she's going to do some Reiki healing... there's something there that she really needs to understand something more... what would that be?*

C: Intuitive medicine... start connecting with more people and... stop hiding behind the wall.

L: *Yes, she's not going to help too many people locking herself away... she needs to connect with more people like herself.*

C: There's something else as well.

L: *She'll know what it is when it comes.*

C: It won't reveal itself now because I'm not ready.

L: *And those spiritual guides and Masters and angels if they were able to give her a message now, what would that be?*

C: Connect with us more... ask for help.

L: *They've definitely been giving help haven't they. Be more open to asking.*

C: But she's now a lot more open to hearing them... so that's good... she's doing good... it's always going to be learning... so it's not like Carla will be fully complete before she starts teaching... and that's another control thing to let go of... you don't have to be perfect before you are someone else's shining light.

L: *Ok, so this journey's going to help her to heal herself and this nutritional plan that she's going to follow... it's going to help her to release a lot of that stuff?*

C: And do it sooner.

L: *So is there anything that she needs to know about... to help her to move into this more purposeful direction.*

C: Just don't be too hard on yourself... the business will come when it's supposed to.

L: *She'll know exactly what to do...*

I asked her how her life would be different now she understood this more fully.

C: It's peaceful now... Life is what you make it.

L: *That's right... you don't need to have those dramas any more.*

C: Just get things done.

It was almost a year after we did the last session that I contacted Carla, I had just finished typing up her case study for this book and I wanted to know how she was doing, how was her health and how did the new relationship turn out. I was a little apprehensive to call because I was worried she may not be doing so well. What follows is the transcribed conversation we had on the phone.

C: I'm doing really well, I'm stable, and feeling great. Did we speak about my new partner in that last session?

L: *Yes, we did, how is that going?*

C: This relationship with Ben has amplified my spiritual progression and also really changed the direction of my business as well, we are very happy. And it's still going; everything is shifting and aligning, running into a very simple fluid life. It's been amazing and I don't even believe I have cancer anymore, it's not something I even talk about or share with anyone and I'm so unidentified with that. I'm also finally able to let my family go on their own journey of whatever that means, instead of trying to control it.

L: *That's fantastic; I'm so pleased for you Carla, how are you going with your studies and your business?*

C: I have been doing a lot of my own informal studies, I have done some training in Reiki and a psychic course as well. I also had a medical intuitive session with a practitioner which was amazing, but through that I realised this type of therapy wasn't exactly where I was meant to be. I feel my calling right now is taking me in a different direction and I am looking forward to where this new path my take me.

L: *The doctors must think your all miracles.*

C: Yes, basically that's what they are saying, they couldn't actually give us any treatment, in the beginning they lined me up for surgery to take out part of my lung, and then chemo but they realised it wouldn't work and withdrew this option. I'm so happy they did that because I'm feeling really good without having had any invasive medical treatment. I have been treating this with a change of diet, fasting and eating only organic food.

L: *Do you remember the predictions that something would happen when you turned 33?*

C: Yes, I'm 33 now and I think this is the time in my live where it all comes together for me, all the pieces of the puzzle fall into place.

When the client is able to forgive during the regression session this can lead to a very powerful session, but forgiveness also needs to be addressed at the conscious level after the session. The phrase, "Forgive and forget" can be meaningless unless this is done. It is necessary to forgive the hurt, but the lesson must be remembered; otherwise, the pattern will continue. The act of forgiveness is processed, primarily, for the healing of the client. It can have very positive effects upon others involved in the original source of the issue as this did with Carla's family. She was able to forgive them and move on.

Forgiveness simply means that the forgiver (client) can be friendly, kind, and cooperative when working with the past offender; however, becoming that person's new best friend is not a requirement. The act of forgiveness puts the original hurt into a healing context and it tries to avoid the possibility of setting up any further scenarios for another victimization. The client strives to avoid both the victim role and the playing of victimizer to another person. There must be no denial that the hurt happened; the lesson must be learned. The valuable aspect of forgiveness work is the severing of chains that link people together in a negative way. Those who are unwilling to forgive others are prisoners of their own hatred. That hatred becomes poison; forgiveness is the antidote. In time, all souls will mature to the realization that forgiveness, both of self and others, has healing qualities.

28. HEALING OF A FRAGMENTED SOUL

AMY'S STORY

"You don't find light by avoiding the darkness."
S. Kelley Harrell

Shamans believe that all illness comes from losing power or giving power away to something or someone. It may be a living person who has an energetic cord attached to you and is sucking part of your soul away. It could be a generational soul loss that happened many years ago with one of your grandfathers or great grandmothers that you are not even aware of that has taken away part of your family soul. Or it could be from past lives where you died from a traumatic experience, or chronic illness or you died a violent death and part of your soul fragmented at your death and remained as an echo or ghost on the earth plain at the location of your death. Any trauma experienced in the past will often cause a part or fragment of energy to remain 'frozen' in the past. This is what Shamans and various indigenous traditions have described as soul loss or soul fragmentation. Working with this 'frozen' part by re-experiencing it, serves to begin to thaw that energy. Once this process begins this part is worked with further to move it into healing, this is in essence, soul retrieval work. One's wholeness must be restored to bring total health and healing of body, mind and spirit back to the client.

The Shaman or Soul Regression Therapist does not use his or her own power to retrieve the lost portion of soul. If he or she did, soon the therapist would be suffering his or her own power depletion. The Shaman uses the spirit animal or ally to travel to the appropriate Inner Worlds to retrieve the soul parts. The spiritual hypnotherapist may use a similar method as the Sharman by using a spirit animal or calling on the assistance of spiritual guides or ancestors and will travel deep into the inner worlds with the intention of retrieving that soul portion that is missing and claim back and redeem all of the parts of our being that have become fragmented or lost. A Soul Regression Therapy past life session can prove effective in this process as it did for my client Amy.

Amy was 26-year-old single woman from Brisbane, she worked as a psychotherapist. During the pre-talk interview, she began to explain that she wanted to find out if the uncomfortable emotional and physical disturbances she experienced at night were from a past life. She said at night she felt terribly and deeply alone along with feelings fear and anxiety especially when she was trying to get to sleep. Amy had experienced many types of therapy in the past but to no avail. Also at night she felt a deep seated, soul level darkness and terror that rise up. She also wanted to know if these feelings were in any way connected to the difficulties she was experiencing with her heart. She explained that she had recently been diagnosed with an ectopic heartbeat. Ectopic heartbeats are small changes in a heartbeat that is otherwise normal. These changes lead to extra or skipped heartbeats, and often there is not a clear cause for these changes.

Amy was a very good hypnotic subject and after only a few minutes she was demonstrating visible signs of being in a very deep hypnotic state. Because Amy was extremely visual and also very in touch with her feelings I decided to use a quicker regression method and take her directly to the cause of the feelings she was experiencing at night.

L: *So what I'd like you to do is think about Sunday night, the last time this woke you up, at 3 o'clock in the morning... remember how it makes you feel physically... shaking... emotionally upset... the feeling of being alone...you feel like you're being abducted... something's happened... someone's taking you... just describe to me perhaps something you hadn't told me before about this feeling... can you tell me a little bit more about that Amy... do you remember the last time this happened?*

A: It feels like they're already in the room... there's something or someone already in the room. And I'm woken because of their presence... it's like my body knows before I do... that there's something not right here.

L: *How does your body respond?*

A: Adrenalin kicks in... my heart rate accelerates, my eyes go wider, and I feel fully alert... it feels like adrenalin.

L: *How was that for you... woken up... heart's racing, you're fully alert... what words would you put around the feelings... what words come to you?*

A: Darkness... it's like immense darkness... there's no light there at all... almost like black magic.

L: *Going into those feelings... it's dark, it's black.*

A: It's like I'm drowning underneath this wave of darkness... and I can breathe and I can't move, and I'm trapped... pinned down... and it's coming.

L: *Going to go back to the source of these feelings... trapped and almost pinned down... something's coming... back to discover what is this... it's ok and safe to find this out.*

A: It's like my hand's being held... I don't know what... 2 people or 1 person... and it's like they're drowning me.

L: *Who are they?*

A: I think they're male... I'm a man.

L: *A man... and you're being held.*

A: By my wrists... they're pushing me down under the water... it's shallow water... someone's gotten a foot over my neck... it's very vicious... they're so angry and aggressive... feel a shoe or boot on my neck... my hand's being held down.

L: *Do you sense you survive this, or not?*

A: I think I do survive this.

L: *You survive it?*

A: Yes, it's like punishment for something... I'm being punished for something but I don't think they want me to die.

L: *Just trying to hold you under?*

A: Yes, it's just a form of control.

At this point in the regression I took Amy back to a younger time to discover what may have caused this to happen. Did she cause something to happen, what did she do? As we continue now.

L: *Where are you now?*

A: I'm tending a field... I don't know what... I've got a long kind of sickle and it's wheat or something... I think I'm a slave.

L: *What colour is your skin?*

A: It's black.

L: *You're in a field... with a sickle?*

A: It's a wheat field and there's a river that runs along the edge of it.

L: *Are there others there with you as well? Or are you on your own.*

A: There are a few.

L: *Are they all males... females?*

A: Some are female... most are male.

L: *What clothes are you wearing?*

A: Like... strange kind of cuffs on my wrists... they're like long... I don't know what they're made out of... and like a white cloth over my legs and groin area... and behind.

L: *What purpose do these cuffs serve?*

A: I don't know.

L: *Do they bind you... are you chained or something?*

A: They're used to bind us.

L: *Are you free at the moment?*

A: No I have chains.

L: *Where are the chains?*

A: On my ankles.

L: *And are there others there that are in charge of you... that give you orders or instructions?*

A: Yes, but they're not... they don't have to be present with us... it's like they are in the sky. They... they're so much more powerful than we are... they're just bigger and stronger and more intelligent... they don't need to be on the ground to control us... they've taken us and now they are using us to farm or to do things... they actually... it's strange... they're in the sky... in ships in the sky... watching us all the time.

L: *And do you ever see them?*

A: Yes.

L: *Can you describe how they look; do they look human?*

A: No.

L: *How do they look?*

A: They're very big... very tall... huge actually... much, much bigger than we are.

L: *How do they communicate with you?*

A: They send images into our brains.

L: *Looking around you... where is this place?*

A: I don't know. I think it's earth... feels like earth... these creatures are not from earth... and it's like they permeate everything in our... like they can see inside me... like they own every inch of me... like I don't even have a soul to call my own... they're in such control... technology that's just beyond what we know... but there's like a house... a building in the distance and I know that's where we all live... me and the other people... and we come out... I think we're mining something actually... it's like we're digging... yes. They want something in the earth... they want minerals or something... I don't know... (crying)... but I just feel so frightened and so alone and so enslaved... absolutely every particle within me belongs to them and it's awful.

L: *How did you get to be caught by these people, have you always been enslaved, what happened to you to cause this?*

A: I was born in a village... very dry, in the desert. and I think I had a family... that feels like a really long time ago.

L: *And do you remember how you got from there to where you are now? What happened?*

A: I think I was taken.

L: *Do you remember that day when they came for you... when you were taken away... was it these beings.*

A: It was like machines. I can see them like running in this tunnel that's underground... I'm trying to get away and my friend that's in front of me, he's running too. I'm running and running... it's like I'm just sucked up, like tentacles... just bore down into the ground and take me up... I was little... I was young... I couldn't even comprehend what was happening.

L: *You were just a boy?*

A: Yes. I couldn't understand what was happening at all.

L: *What happened to your family... did they get taken as well?*

A: My little brother, he came with me... I found him... my parents... they were taken, but somewhere else.

I decided to take Amy to the last day of this life, often they will know more about the story of that life once they have gone through the death. Regression is similar to reading a book or watching a movie once we are at the end we can reflect back on the story. We continue the dialogue at this point.

L: *Are you inside or outside.*

A: I'm outside. Looks like there's a fire... I've always had to work in that... on that land in that field... there's... something's happening like there's a... I don't know, it's like a disaster or an earthquake... something... like the ground is shaking and everybody's just running everywhere... chaos... it's almost like the earth is kind of cracking apart.

L: *What happens to you in that last moment?*

A: I pick up a child who's crying... and I run and I run... and we hide for a little bit in like some cave or a tree or something... it's just kind of like... it's almost like war... like a war has broken out... the sky is red... there's smoke everywhere and fire... it feels like not a bad thing though... it feels like perhaps our liberation... it's like they're breaking down. They couldn't continue the way that they were... and it's all coming to an end... like the earth itself is cracking up... like having an earthquake and... sinking down and taking everything with it... and I think I get pulled down there and I die... crushed.

L: *So being be aware as you leave that body of what you are thinking and feeling... as you take that last breath.*

A: I'm so angry... angry and upset... I feel like... like I always have faith... in... faith in the light... and yet there was so much darkness that prevailed over my life that I feel very angry about that... I feel like I was abandoned... like I was deserted by the light.

As Amy passes and moves away from the body in that physical life she begins to feel the freedom that many clients feel at this stage. They often report feeling light and free as they float in a soul state above the body they once occupied. As we continue.

L: *As you move into that beautiful state of peace now... just release the body and look around... where are you now. Is it light or dark around you?*

A: It's very light... very beautiful.

L: *What do you feel now?*

A: I feel very peaceful... very calm... expanded and just kind of endless... and I feel like there's a lot of love here.

L: *Is there anyone there to meet you... or do you have a sense of seeing others there?*

A: There's lots of beings... guides... other spirits... they recognise me straight away and they come to me and they just embrace me.

L: *They're pleased to see you again... that darkness is behind you, and you're now in the light.*

A: Yes, it feels like a really wonderful reunion.

Amy enjoys this reunion and special connection with these beings of light. She begins to telepathically connect to a spokesperson that can help her to understand what that lifetime was about.

A: I don't know if this makes sense but the first thing that came through is I'm to learn how to be in control of your own life.

L: *To learn to be in control of your own life.*

A: Yes, and I'm saying, well I was completely controlled that whole life... what was the point?

L: *Where was that life lived, was it earth or was it another place? There's many realms, dimensions.*

A: Yes, it was another place... another planet.

L: *Was that life the one before Amy, Or further back? It affected her in her current life, waking her in the night with fears and terror.*

A: I'm just asking.

L: *What's the first thought or message that comes in?*

A: Yes, it was.

L: *The last life.*

A: Yes.

L: *On another planet somewhere. And you lived that life so you could learn to be in control even though you were out of control. So how do they think you went, what does your guide have to say about that?*

A: Someone's saying you needed to learn how to be yourself... to be true to yourself.

L: *When you died in that life you were so angry. Such a dark, controlled life.*

A: I just asked what did I gain from that and they said strength.

L: *Strength?*

A: It's like it touched me on such a deep soul level I would never allow myself to be in that situation again.

L: *So how does this connect to Amy's life. She won't allow herself ever to be controlled by anyone?*

A: I'm getting this issue is pushing up and out and through... because it needs manifestation in this life...

L: *And how can that help Amy... what does Amy need to know about it... what does she need to do?*

A: Anchor that element on a soul level.

L: *What is it that Amy needs to learn?*

A: I need to learn how to move through it.

L: *What is it that Amy needs to learn to move through?*

A: The darkness.

L: *So what can she do to move through this, what does she need to do in her current life?*

A: To overcome a fear of control.

L: *And how does that fear of being controlled affect Amy? She's frightened and it holds her back in some way.*

A: She's to relinquish control and to just flow with life.

L: *She finds this difficult to do?*

A: Parts of her do.

L: *I'm wondering... is this a lesson, to learn to let go, to flow with life? Is this a lesson that she's been learning over more lives than just these lives we've seen including the life on the other planet as the man, how many other lives has she's lived where she's been learning to let go, to flow with life?*

A: 7.

L: *7 lives, what is the deeper truth of this now, is it to just let go, not try to control so much?*

A: Trust.

L: *Trust that it's ok to let go?*

A: Trust that it's ok to be open. She thinks that if she's open it will happen again?

L: *People will try to control her?*

A: She'll be taken and controlled, yes... enslaved.

L: *Enslaved... so those other lives... the 7... do they include the lives as Amy and the man on the other planet. Or there are 7 others?*

A: Yes.

I move into Soul Regression Therapy at this point and connect with the other past lives. There was a mixture of male and female lives. One of the female past lives was as a prostitute this is where we re-join the session.

A: There's a female in like a corset and long petticoats and skirts... with her hair tied up... I don't know... 1700s or 1800s kind of dress... green and black... with like black boots... like cabaret or something... in London I think.

L: *And how did this enslavement... this woman that you were... how did this affect her, was she controlled in some way?*

A: She was a prostitute. And there was a lot of violence in her life and a lot of abuse... physical, emotional, sexual abuse... she's so tired... deathly tired.

L: *And how did she die... what happened to her?*

A: From a fall... she fell... falling out of something... I don't know what... a building or something... off a building. Looks like a very busy, overcrowded kind of city... little cobblestone alleyways and streets, and like an inn.

L: *Was she young or older when she died?*

A: She was middle aged... 40 something.

L: *Was she still working as a prostitute?*

A: Yes, Diana was her name... Dianne.

L: *What about the other past life characters?*

A: There's somebody else... it's hard for me to see him properly... he's got like a top hat and he keeps twirling it... and like bowing... like he's an entertainer or a dancer or something... he was in the circus or something like that... I think this was in France.

L: *And how was his life in the circus?*

A: I don't know... he just says I was just so unhappy... he would work and he was a good entertainer... he was good at what he did... I don't know what he did... he was very unhappy... very depressed... drank a lot... disillusioned... and I think he killed himself actually.

L: *What about the others? They had similar lives.*

A: So there's some sort of cowboy... he was hung... he was hung in the gallows... I don't know what he did... something... he couldn't rest.

L: *Couldn't rest... he was always on the run.*

A: Yes... he was caught and hanged.

L: *What did he do, why were they chasing him?*

A: Someone lassoed him around the neck... and snapped his neck... pulled him off his horse... he was running away... from... I don't know... enemies.

L: *Allow yourself to know what this is, weaving between these lives that you lived. Is it being enslaved?*

A: It's being in situations where I felt powerless... creating lives where I feel completely powerless and at the mercy of something stronger, higher.

L: *Stronger force?*

A: Yes, force or person or circumstance. because they're all so filled with violence and pain and anguish... and there's always that sense of powerlessness and of deprivation... it's like all these pieces are all wounds in my soul... they're all kind of contributing to this... density and this disturbance now... they're all kind of crying for release... they're all unresolved.

All of these past lives, upon death carried with them unresolved emotions, a theme of anger, betrayal, enslavement, themes that were still repeating in Amy's current incarnation. As we continued the therapy resolution Amy became aware that these lives were unconscious, unaware of how what their unresolved karma was and how it was affecting Amy. These past lives had become fragmented and so one after another Amy gathered all the fragments of the emotional trauma connected to each past life and returned them each to the afterlife. These in fact were all aspects/ fragments of Amy's soul that were left behind undealt with in previous incarnations. Once she had completed this task and all the fragments were once again bought back to the light and restored the essence of these past lives gathered around as we pick up the dialogue once again.

L: *And they're there all around you, surrounding you know, feeling whole again, and they're all going to be just fine... your guides are there and they're all helping to heal... all those pieces are being placed back within the soul of you... all that energy now. So how does that feel now?*

A: It feels good.

L: *The soul becomes whole again. Reconnecting to who you are as a soul. You lived those lives... you experienced those events... but you survived it all because you are here... you're Amy, and you've learnt from it... and that's what it's about... learning... and they're all going to be just fine. They all go off to where they need to be, and I'm wondering now if your guide has anything for you... to take you anywhere... to speak with you more?*

A: He's telling me that I did a good job, and giving me a hug... and just smiling at me.

L: *That's right... you did a good job... as a soul you chose those lives because you thought you were up for it... your guide says you did a good job. So how do you feel about your life now as Amy, how is this going to help you now that you've understood these lives that you've lived.*

A: I feel like more whole and more at peace and more light from inside of me.

L: *It's coming from inside?*

A: There's no fear here.

L: *No, because you are from the light and you might see other beings there... and I'm just wondering if they're members of your soul family... perhaps souls that you've previously lived lives with or who are perhaps in your current life. Do you sense or see any others there?*

A: Yes, there's a very tall, big, sort of strong man... don't know who he is... and I feel my grandmothers are here... one of my grandmothers.

L: *Do they have any messages for you... does grandmother have any messages for you?*

A: She said don't be afraid.

L: *As she says that to you now, how do you feel?*

A: Good.

L: *Yes, they're there... they're watching over you.*

A: She said I'm much stronger than I give myself credit for.

L: *You do have that strength. You've been learning to be strong by living those lives. And now you understand it... you are a light being and are here to help others, perhaps. What is your soul purpose, you've come through all these lives... what is your purpose?*

A: One of them says to be yourself.

L: *What does Amy need to do to become more herself?*

A: Follow my gut, and follow my heart.

L: *Was that something that you found difficult to do in the past?*

A: Yes.

L: *And how do you feel, about being more able to do that?*

Are you more attuned with your inner self now?

A: Yes, definitely.

L: *So is there anything else... any other messages, or any other place that you'd like to visit?*

A: There's something coming through... a woman stepping through... I'm not really sure why... and she's standing in front of me... she's got kind of like a long white dress on and a big headdress... actually looks Egyptian... and she wants to show me something...

L: *And what does she show you?*

A: We're going like out of a dwelling... down steps... going down into the earth, like a cave... I can hear water dripping somewhere and I can smell rock... it's a very sacred place... she's telling me to put my hands on the wall.

L: *How does that feel as you put your hands on the wall?*

A: This is where it feels like it's like I'm almost sinking into it. It's like a portal or something. And then when I sink into it actually I come out and there's stars everywhere... like I'm in the sky... and she's kind of floating around me and she's saying 'This is where your family is... this is where you belong'... or 'this is where you come from', or something.

L: *It's where you come from... from the stars?*

A: It's safe... and I need to use more of my gifts from where I come from. There's a lot of light here and I need to channel it more... through myself into my life... into my work.

L: *So what advice does she have for you... how can you tap into this energy... to use your special gift?*

A: She says I'm very special... and that I was born to do great things...

L: *Will Amy automatically be able to tap into this healing energy to help other people?*

A: If I hold her in my being, yes, always. I think this is Isis. She will work through me... She's like pulled me close... and, you know, like 'don't forget' or 'return here'... 'return to me' or 'my bosom' almost... "because that's where you're safe... that's where I will remember my own power'.

L: *Have you had an Egyptian life... where you've used this power?*

A: Yes. Many times. I've been there quite a few times. I was an initiate in the temple and a high priestess... the secrets of the universe were unfolded to me... I held them... I held the template for them.

L: *So what happened... your soul chose to live some very different lives, very hard lives after this, what caused your soul to change lives or lessons, experiences?*

A: There were still parts that were dark and not manifested... there were still parts in shadow that needed to be lived, to be expressed, and then therefore evolved... I needed to have those physical manifestations in order to evolve those parts of myself and bring them to the light.

L: *Which you've done now.*

A: Yes.

L: *So you have these gifts within you... you've lived magical lives where you've been powerful, and you understand the secrets of the universe... you've had that template... so when you think of Isis and you connect to her now... perhaps you can tap back into the source of that energy and it can help you in your current life as Amy, is that something you can do?*

A: Yes, definitely.

L: *Do you feel you have direction now?*

A: Yes.

L: *So does Isis have any further messages for you?*

A: She said 'My child you are my beloved and I shall protect you for all the days that your soul exists'.

L: *Sounds like she's really working with you and you can tune into her energy. What are you going to do differently now... to ensure that your life continues on a more appropriate course for the development of your soul?*

A: I'm going to just trust and know that all I have to do is flow with life and know that I'm protected and know that I'm safe.

Conclusion

This was a very powerful session for Amy she gained a lot of insights as to why she felt so very scared, alone and anxious at night. Amy discovered that she was still experiencing the feelings of the life she lived as the slave. Because there was so much darkness and terror that prevailed over that life she had brought some of it with her, also anger and feelings of being abandoned, but the abandonment was from the source or the light as she called this.

She discovered that one of her lessons was to learn to be in control of her own life. Her soul was really pushing her to resolve this issue by manifestation in this life. To overcome the fear of being controlled she needs to relinquish control and to just flow with life. To trust that it's ok to be open, she had thought that if she allowed herself to be open to a relationship she would be opening herself up to be controlled again, or enslaved.

She looked at few other lives with a similar theme, a tragic life as Dianne, a prostitute in the 1700s or 1800's. In this life she experienced more violence, enslavement and abuse. Another unhappy life emerged as a French male entertainer who worked in a circus. He was very depressed, drank a lot and became disillusioned with life, he suicided.

Another life emerged as a cowboy who was hung at the gallows. He was always on the run and eventually was caught and hanged. Amy realised she had lived many lives where she had been in situations of feeling completely powerless and at the mercy of some stronger force that controlled her, which eventually lead to death. Many lives filled with violence, pain and anguish, with a sense of powerlessness and of deprivation. Amy said, "it's like all these pieces are wounds in my soul, contributing to this density and disturbance in my life now. They are all crying for release, they are all unresolved. When I died the last time... it's like there was this thread... this cord... even though I was in the afterlife... in the light... I was still so connected to the emotion of that life... that anger... intense anger and feelings of being betrayed and just desperation... and it's like all these cords to these unresolved emotions that are all sitting here. It's like they're all still in purgatory so to speak."

Amy's description above is exactly how people feel when their soul has been fragmented and split over many life times of trauma. As the session progressed Amy began to understand that she has special gifts and she can automatically tap into this healing energy to help herself and other people. She connected to the Archetypal energy of Isis and realised that Isis will work through her. The reason for the session was to connect to the dark and un-manifested parts of her soul that were in shadow that needed to be lived, to be expressed, and then therefore evolved. She realised that she needed to have those physical manifestations/past lives in order to evolve those parts of herself and bring them to the light. That she could now just trust and know that all she has to do is flow with life and know that she is protected and safe. We were able to get to the core of her problems from this session and heal her soul wounds by reconnecting to her true immortal soul essence.

29. IN CONCLUSION

We were originally drawn to work in the field of hypnotic past life regression because we were looking for proof of the survival of the soul after death. We have to date regressed thousands of clients back to remember their past lives and to understand their immortal soul's journey which lead many of them to obtain relief from present day physical pain, illnesses, emotional problems and phobias. We have now ceased attempting to prove the reality of past lives because we are no longer concerned with proof, this is not the goal for therapeutic past life regression.

What is most important is the facilitation of therapy which helps the client to understand the complexities of what's coming from past life memory into the current life and enables the client to unravel these memories in their own unique way and understand the differences between them. Change does not just result from learning about the past life storyline, story content, or story outcome. Change results from the retrieving and linking of experiences in past lives and the current life. This assists the client to self-realization which leads to the integration of themselves more completely on a conscious and soul level, when this occurs, magic happens and the client's problems gradually dissipate.

We created the Soul Regression Therapy 6 day facilitators training course so that we could teach a method of spiritual regression therapy that is unique, our mission statement is:

Our mission is to awaken consciousness and facilitate the

healing of Souls globally through building a network of enlightened healers.

A question that we are asked a lot is, "if we have past lives, why do we not remember them?" Most people don't really give much thought to the fact that we also forget significant parts of our present lives. Most of us cannot remember learning to walk or learning to read and write. Imagine if we remembered every little detail about our present lives, the mind would be so cluttered it would be difficult to concentrate on the present. The amazing thing is that our past memories don't disappear altogether; they are tucked away inside our subconscious mind, current life and past lives. This can be compared to being stored on a cyber cloud; they are accessible with the aid of a skilled regression therapist.

There is a huge shift towards energy work and spiritually based therapy and many people are ready to release karmic patterns and complexes, and unfortunately main stream therapies are proving less than effective with this. The Earth is changing its vibration and frequency; we are preparing to move into a new vibratory consciousness, a new era. Because of this shift many people are waking up to the realisation there is more to who they are, that life is not what they thought. This is leading them to seek help to discover who they really are and their soul's purpose. Most problems are based in a past-life cause, even when they appear to be resulting from current-life issues, such as trauma, fears, habits or conflicts. Soul Regression Therapy helps find the cause. Only when you know what really set the situation into motion can you generate a full release.

"Self-realization means that we have been consciously connected with our source of being. Once we have made this connection, then nothing can go wrong". Swami Paramananda.

Authors

Lorna and John Jackson are known as qualified leaders in the field of Past Life Regression and Between Lives Hypnotherapy in Australia, they are internationally recognised as the co-creators of the pioneering healing modality "Soul Regression Therapy". They have trained extensively in the areas of Hypnotherapy, Psychotherapy, Healing Techniques, and Regression Therapies with many of the worlds pioneers in these fields. Their passion and interest has always been in Past Lives and the immortal Souls journey, exploring their own Past Lives and wanting to help others do the same. They are qualified and certified, practising Clinical Regression Hypnotherapists, and TNI Certified Life Between Lives Hypnotherapists. They have operated their renowned private practice in Brisbane and the Gold Coast since 2004. Both John and Lorna are gifted visionaries having guided thousands of people through regression to self-discovery and to understand their true immortal identity. They are also the founders and Directors of Training at The Jackson Institute, Australia. The mission of The Jackson Institute is to help awaken consciousness and facilitate the healing of souls globally through building a network of enlightened healers.

Over the many years of their work they have compiled a large body of reincarnation evidence and research. They co-created their own training program and process "Soul Regression Therapy", which is taught as a 6-day facilitator's course, and is open to therapists and non-therapists alike. This course is taught around Australia and internationally. Lorna has written many articles about past life regression and the afterlife that have been published in Australian. They train, lecture and are regular speakers at spiritual churches and gatherings, having attended spiritual expos, afterlife conferences and events over the years, speaking about their work.

For more information about this book, Soul Regression Therapy training course or about Lorna and Johns work, go to:

www.soulregressiontherapy.com.au
www.spiritualregression.com.au

ACKNOWLEDGEMENTS

To begin I would like to acknowledge our clients who have given permission for their case studies to be used in this book, without them there would be no subject matter to write about. I would like to extend my heartfelt gratitude to my husband and soul mate John Jackson for his unwavering contribution, encouragement, support, suggestions, inspiration in developing and editing the manuscript during the writing of this book.

My sincere thanks go out to Maria Delaney for transcribing audio recordings of the case study sessions used in this book. I would also like to thank my publishing company "Publicious" for producing this book. Last but not least I would like to thank our beautiful canine soul companion Dexter for his company over the many hours spent at my computer.